W9-BON-801

WITHDRAWN

The Revenge of the Real

The Revenge of the Real

Politics for a Post-pandemic World

BENJAMIN BRATTON

LA GRANGE PUBLIC LIBRARY
10 W. COSSITT AVE.
LA GRANGE, IL 60525
708-215-3200

V

VERSO

London • New York

3 1320 00523 3213

AUG - '21

First published by Verso 2021
© Benjamin Bratton 2021

All rights reserved

The moral rights of the author have been asserted

1 3 5 7 9 10 8 6 4 2

Verso
UK: 6 Meard Street, London W1F 0EG
US: 20 Jay Street, Suite 1010, Brooklyn, NY 11201
versobooks.com

Verso is the imprint of New Left Books

ISBN-13: 978-1-83976-256-7
ISBN-13: 978-1-83976-259-8 (US EBK)
ISBN-13: 978-1-83976-258-1 (UK EBK)

British Library Cataloguing in Publication Data
A catalogue record for this book is available from the British Library

Library of Congress Cataloging-in-Publication Data
A catalog record for this book is available from the Library of Congress

Typeset in Monotype Fournier by Hewer Text UK Ltd, Edinburgh
Printed in the UK by CPI Group (UK) Lrd, Croydon CR0 4YY

614.4
BRA

CONTENTS

ACKNOWLEDGMENTS

This book began as part of the "Revenge of the Real" project of the Terraforming think tank at the Strelka Institute in Moscow. As COVID-19 crept across the globe, and after our researchers scattered back to their countries of passport, we trained our thoughts on the pandemic convulsing global culture. Many of the ideas herein were first ventured in the essay "18 Lessons of Quarantine Urbanism," published on April 3, 2020, by *Strelka Mag*.

Preface:
WHEN DEATH GOVERNS LIFE

This is a book about how societies govern life and death, how they fail and succeed, and how the COVID-19 pandemic made clear that the planetary society we need is one that embraces this responsibility. It is also about how so much philosophy failed the pandemic's test, and so provides an outline for an alternative. A successful response to a pandemic, or to climate change, or to how we care for one another, should be "biopolitical" in a *positive* sense. It is literally a matter of life and death.

The most difficult lessons to be learned are those that come when *reality*—in the form of a virus, of our vulnerability to it, of our inadequate governing responses to it—crashes through comforting illusions and ideologies.

This book is published at a time that is hopefully closer to the end of the pandemic than to the beginning, a moment when change is necessary and seems possible. Recognizing the lessons of "the revenge of the real," it envisions a post-pandemic politics and what must happen now. Can the world govern itself differently? If so, what models are needed?

Paul Preciado writes, "Tell me how your community constructs its political sovereignty and I will tell you what forms your plagues will take." Yes, and the inverse is equally and painfully true, especially when sovereignty is defined by its absence. This pandemic demonstrates a critical inability of the West, in particular, to govern itself as it needs to.

Coronaviruses are ancient. We and they co-evolved. The real culprit is not, as some have suggested, an unnatural global entanglement that can be undone by blunt segregation, putting everyone and everything back in place. Entanglement is the baseline, not the exception.

The pandemic has revealed dire inadequacies not just in state responses, but in the political cultures that credentialize, shape, and reflect them. The reason one country succeeded where another one failed is not only the different policies but also the different cultures that accept or reject those policies in the first place. What worked in Taiwan may be unacceptable in Italy or Texas.

We must understand post-pandemic politics both in terms of how the state interacts with society as well as in terms of how a human society that is utterly planetary in scope knows itself, models itself, and attempts to compose, organize, and care for itself through various mechanisms, be they public, personal, private, or scientific.

The anarchic state of international politics in which nations close off from one another and compete for resources such as data or vaccines—when it needn't be a zero-sum game—is both unnecessary and dangerously uncoordinated. It puts all of us in a position where common problems exist at a planetary scale but are addressed at a local scale that is comparatively myopic. The governance challenges of climate change parallel this situation. Sooner rather than later, something must and will give.

With that future in mind, this book holds as a matter of principle that to advance a scientific biological conception of life is not to *reduce* the world to mere facts, but to recognize its complexity and fragility, and therefore that it also can't be reduced to the constructed meanings we might project upon it. The pandemic is a *revenge of the real*. It is a non-negotiable reality that upends comfortable illusions, no matter how hard some may try to push back with their chosen form of magic.

What are the forms of "the real" that the pandemic has forced us to confront? How has the unprecedented filtering and sorting of people into their countries of passport revealed the power and limits of exclusive national citizenship? How will the epidemiological view of society and collective risk alter the commonsense notion of what a "society" is? What lessons must be learned from how different governments responded to the virus, successfully or catastrophically, for what comes next? How does the uneven and inequitable distribution of testing and care demonstrate just how collective the risk really is, and also put into question simplistic dismissals of all forms of technological sensing as pernicious "surveillance"?

What do the "mask wars" reveal about the destructive (and self-destructive) nature of libertarian individualism as the basis of sovereignty? As we pass by a stranger, how do the ethics of the immunological commons shift from subjective intention of harm or endearment to the objective biological circumstance of contagion? Is it at all surprising that the philosophies based on "biopolitical critique," which hold that any governance of bodies is fundamentally authoritarian and illegitimate, fail so miserably in interpreting what is truly at stake? In turn, as the communities first to implement lockdowns began to open back up, what did the explosion of protests against police violence reveal about the effects of a generational dismantling of equitable, effective governance?

Finally, what now for post-pandemic Earth? In a rational and equitable world, what forms of planetary protection, governance, and *competence* are needed, and what deep and difficult changes in political culture might bring them about? Can the West learn some obvious lessons, or not?

There is nothing easy on offer, no simple solutions. The book doesn't offer much in the way of feel-good sonnets about good guys and bad guys that imply more explanation than they actually provide. The stakes are too deep and too wide. The reality of the situation is genuinely disorienting, including for some of our most esteemed cultural theorists. Where aesthetic resistance to vertical planning and scientific rationality was often seen as progressive, we are confronted with a reality in which intuitive individualism in the guise of "health freedom" is now widely understood as dangerous. The ground has rotated, making some previously obscured paths more open and clearer.

The post-pandemic politics I describe is one that is inclusive, materialist, restorative, rationalist, and based on a more demystified image of the human species, anticipating a future different from the one prescribed by many cultural traditions. It accepts the evolutionary entanglement of mammals and viruses. It accepts death as part of life. It therefore accepts the responsibilities of medical knowledge to prevent and mitigate unjust deaths and misery, as something quite different from the nativist immunization of one population of people from another. It is *biopolitics* in a positive and projective sense. Whatever the outcomes, they are deliberate, by action or by inaction. Laissez-faire vitalism for which "life will find a way" is not an option; it is a fairy tale. Similarly, pretending that biopower should not exist, and that choices concerning what does and does not live can be evaded because they are difficult and disturbing, is ultimately another way of allowing biopower to be exercised without accountability.

This book's analysis, diagnosis, and prescriptions will undoubtedly seem to some to call for a model of governance based on planetary-scale technological rationalism. They are not wrong; it does, but there is more to it than that. It is an attempt to use the pandemic as a lens into the deeper issues that allow us to imagine a world in which planetary society is able to deliberately compose itself with compassion and reason. This means letting go of the idea that such a composition can emerge entirely on its own any more than a sick body can be healed by just letting life and death take their course.

The book was written over a matter of weeks and is meant as a timely polemic rather than a definitive statement. There is much more that needs to be said that I couldn't say in these pages. For example, there is more to say on the role and function of economics, and why, at least in the West, both corporate systems driven by short-term profits and sclerotic state bureaucracies are ill-equipped to meet the moment. Asia's comparatively effective responses present a different story on both counts, and that difference represents what is of concern.

This book is a cultural critique or, more accurately, a critique of Western political culture and its present philosophical shortcomings. This is not because I believe culture and philosophy are separate from and more important than biology and epidemiology, but rather because I do not.

I

THE REVENGE OF THE REAL

It is difficult, if not impossible, to offer commentary on a quickly shifting situation. One can assume what the outcome may be but, as ever, the most likely outcome is almost never what actually happens. Allow me then to provide a little context with reference to the current signposts.

Today, Western countries are in various stages of lockdown, catastrophe, and contradiction, while China is tentatively opening up again after months of hardship. In the United States, where I am holed up, the government fumbles between incoherent phases of bluster and hedging. Friends who should know better are turning into the conspiracist Jude Law plays in the 2011 film *Contagion*. Spanning the globe, the Kübler-Ross stages of grief are the new national horoscope: denial, anger, bargaining, depression, acceptance. To say that the United States is ten days behind Italy is not only an epidemiological analysis; it is a psychiatric diagnosis.

We are looking at months more of extreme weirdness and grief and then things will return to a state that will feel more normal, but forever not the same normal. Right now, that is the optimistic scenario. Afterward, many ways of doing things, ways of thinking, ways of getting things going may just not come back. Some will be missed, others not even noticed. What are the important lessons to be learned before the normality that caused so much mayhem returns? Yet another "second wave" of the virus would be catastrophic, but so would another wave of its underlying causes.

The sense of emergency is palpable and real. But instead of naming this moment a "state of exception," we should see it more as revealing *pre-existing conditions*. The consequences of poor planning (or no planning), broken social systems, and isolationist reflexes are explicit. Vigilance should not be maintained against the "emergency" on behalf of familiar norms, but against those dysfunctional norms returning after the coast is declared clear. We must keep attention trained on the pathologies revealed, and in doing so willfully inhabit a changed world and its many challenges.

For post-pandemic politics, this should be a deathblow to the reactionary forms of political populism of recent years, which were built on simple, cathartic stories of resentment and recrimination. But will that be the case? It is not remotely certain. The pandemic (and climate change and many other things besides) makes clear that the present anarchic state of geopolitics must give way to forms of governance that are equitable, effective, rational and therefore realist. If nothing else, this book is a call for a new realist form of planetary politics as an antidote to the populist incoherency of recent years that is clearly not up to the task. "Populism" is herein defined not as the political and/or cultural project of the working class, but by its more specific connotations of demagoguery, folksy scapegoating, simplistic emotional appeals, fearmongering and boundary policing, empty theatrics and sham symbolism, charisma-driven grifts, and so on.

This mode of populism, which has successfully led candidates into executive and legislative power over the past several years, despises expertise and fetishizes metaphors. To address the pandemic, however, people require competence. At this moment, when those who said the virus was a hoax now suggest it should simply run its inevitable course, a dry, well-planned, trustworthy, available, adaptable, responsive, forward-looking approach seems like the program of the most idealistic politics imaginable. Yet the human ability to bend facts to favored narratives remains incredible. The varied responses to the global contagion by different societies have exposed many ideologies and traditions as ineffective, fraudulent, and suicidal.

In some countries, we see extreme examples where the speech of the sovereign executive is taken as the literal last word on whether the virus exists, what it means, who started it, what should be administered in response, all adding up to not just a politics of loyalty but a high-resolution alternate reality. This populism is symptomatic of a generational dismantling of public systems and international cooperation. In the name of markets or bottom-up cooperation, societies have been left with little but increasingly pathologic forms of "emergence." As the spine breaks, the general response is to attack the very idea of governance on behalf of a yet more emphatic spontaneity. This is not unexpected. Populism thrives because of a sense that the system is broken, and to be sure, it is, but not in the ways that populists believe it is and not in the ways that demagogues preach it.

In this light, populism is a form of anti-governance. It sees not only that the levers of power are corrupt or incompetent in specific ways, but that they are illegitimate in vague and general ways, and so its response is also vague and general, as well as immediate, visceral, and uncomplicated. As a basis for any possible biopolitics, it eschews direct pragmatic engagement with reality because it is a prisoner of its emotional investments. This is how statues of war heroes can command more earnest defense than the bodies of living people, how viral memes of celebrity bodies can break the internet, and how spin and disinformation are able to create culturally complete artificial worlds that people endow with their hope, fear, and rage. That is, populism subordinates the repairing of broken systems to a virtual contest of semiotic brinkmanship.

In the same way that Institutional Critique is actually the last vestige of faith in the authority of art institutions, the aestheticized politics of populism can wrap itself so tightly in the rituals and ornaments of power and resistance to power that power itself can watch from a safe distance. Finally, the populist politics that set the stage for the West's inadequate response to the virus remains stuck in a world where politics means to oppose, change, police, or defend the *representation* of the real, often with contempt for the very idea that the underlying reality may be utterly indifferent.

This is why the COVID-19 pandemic is *a revenge of the real* making itself known. Its unresponsiveness to the endemic Canutism upon which our current politics depends is the crucial lesson around which post-pandemic politics must be formed. Just as King Canute is said to have stood before the waves and commanded them to stop, today's populists are beholden to a faith in the power of their own gestures. But the pandemic is an irruptive revelation of the complex biological reality of the planet with which we are entangled, and that underlying reality is apathetic to the plotlines and mythic lessons we may try to project upon it. This does not mean we cannot know it, grasp it, make sense of it, model and respond to it, and change it *as it is*. We can. In the most fundamental sense, this is the definition of the governance that should have animated pandemic politics and should guarantee post-pandemic politics.

It should also animate post-pandemic philosophy. This, too, failed the moment, sometimes with willful ignorance, incoherent expressions of powerlessness, and sometimes outright intellectual fraud. It is a shame because many of the necessary and needed concepts are already at hand. We know more than we realize, and so in this way the revenge of the real is also a return of the repressed. Repressed are the biological realities of human society's co-evolution with viruses, the epidemiological reality of populations, the real calculus of positive and negative freedom all on behalf of various placebos—chief among them, as I will argue, are myths of individual *autonomy*.

Perhaps the most important reality once repressed and now returning is that of a social realm neglected after years of the dismantling of all forms of public governance—all except for police functions, that is. This reality, along with the thermal pressure of a widespread lockdown, led to protests and a *social explosion*, one that demystified illusions about who is and is not fully part of society and in what ways. A series of regularized biological and social deaths became turning points, and with them a return of the principle of breakdown. The question is, what comes next?

As said, the book's argument is on behalf a "positive biopolitics" that may form the basis of viable social self-organization, but this is less a statement on behalf of "the political" in some metaphysical sense than on behalf of a *governmentality* through which an inevitably planetary society can deliberately compose itself. If contemporary philosophy's often reactionary suspicions have backed it into the corner where it can conceive of "biopolitics" only as a totalitarian oppression in need of endless critique and constant dismantling, then it needs a refresher course and a gut check. Waves of Boomers, myself included, grew up in a world in which the bad establishment was (supposedly) hierarchical and rationalist and, therefore, individualism and autonomy and spontaneous irrationality were (supposedly) a position of resistance, but we all find ourselves awake in a world where that opposition appears severely bent if not wholly inverted. Today our hospitals and morgues are full because of the horizontal, spontaneous, individualist irrationality of the status quo.

Why is the West's response shambolic, and what is the positive biopolitical alternative? The touchpoints that comprise the argument are varied. They involve the right to be counted and the role of sensing to ensure the likelihood of equitable models of ourselves. Those models are understood as the basis of a recursive self-composition of society, not just surveillant policing representations. The problem of over-individuation, then, is the crux of my critique of surveillance culture but also of the overinflation of the term "surveillance" to dismiss all modes of social sensing as pernicious violations.

Furthermore, what is truly "essential" about certain kinds of work and workers? How does urban-scale automation and its relays of people, software, and goods enable both social cohesion across great chains of mediation and social occlusion of its actual, underlying mechanisms? Considering the masks on our faces, how is Ethics overly dependent upon notions of subjective intention when the real collective risk has little to do with intent of harm or goodwill but with physical proximity? *Why* has the philosophy of biopolitics so vociferously limited its engagement with scientific biology to the realms of "discourse" and seen it primarily as a tool of control, and how did that cripple its ability to offer enough useful ideas during the pandemic? Finally, what constitutes the forms of planetary *competency* through which we might support ourselves?

Mid-pandemic, it could not be more excruciatingly clear that a biopolitics of population-scale self-composition and realist care must be constructed at the scale of the planetary population itself. Through this, we, the *Homo sapiens* in biological aggregate, might remake our settlements in the image of our interdependencies and aspirations. "Medicare for All" is a creakingly quaint vision compared to what is possible.

Lastly, post-pandemic politics is not a simple set of programmatic beliefs. It is not explainable by a colored pill (red pill, blue pill, black pill, and so on), that is, a complete master narrative and source of identity in the discrete form of a virtual pharmaceutical pellet. What is required is instead an acceptance of how the rapid intrusion of an indifferent reality can make wholly symbolic resistance worse than futile. There is no simple formula that will work. We have to build a politics capable of engagement with the full complexity of reality. The pre-existing conditions that have now been exposed clarify the need for a geopolitics based not on self-undermining, prisoner's dilemma tactics in the face of common risks, but on a deliberate plan for the coordination of the planet we occupy and make and re-make over again. Otherwise, this moment will be an unnecessarily permanent emergency.

But first, what happened?

2

THE BIG FILTERING

All of you have spent the pandemic in different places, to various degrees locked down. Among the issues that post-pandemic politics must account for is what states did during the crisis, how the virus moved from city to city, country to country, population to population, and specifically what the pandemic did with and to the idea of citizenship.

Where did everyone go? Among the most decisive and disturbing realities of the pandemic was a big filtering whereby whole populations of people, otherwise mobile and intermingling, were *re-sorted back into their countries of passport*, often with only a few days' notice.

The re-filtering and re-sorting of people into constituent national categories of citizenship is a primary sociological fact of this pandemic: Americans have been filtered back into the United States, Indians filtered back into India, South Koreans filtered back into South Korea, Brazilians filtered back into Brazil. The physical organization of people according to formal citizenship (or legal residence) and their place within the post-colonial national political order is something we observe with trepidation in light of what it ultimately implies about our ability to address shared problems.

It serves to put us each in place, one where we are bound not only to our own personal experiences of this moment, but also to the official political response to the crisis by our country of passport. Access to important resources is therefore conditional or arbitrary and depends on where you happen to be standing when the music stops. Those sent back to Florida face a very different biopolitical reality than, for example, those sent back to Singapore or New Zealand.

The big filtering also leads to many seemingly unlikely episodes and exceptions. By late spring, people were trying to get back *into* China by any means necessary to escape the virus and the incompetent responses of particular Western countries. New Zealand's status as the preferred backup plan of the "doomsday prepper" class was validated and affirmed. Mexico closed its borders with the United States to disallow the contagious Americans from infecting them. Barbados is still offering a special pandemic visa for those willing and able to wait it out on the beaches.

As the global population was sorted this way because no other option seemed available, the weaknesses and capacities of nationalism in the broadest sense were apparent. What else could have been? Fixing the right of entry and movement to a state identity certificate is a historically recent development, one based on the separation of migrants from natives and the establishment of exclusive citizenship as a condition of movement. There is nothing necessary or obvious about this as our default setting. That there was no other apparent option is an indictment of our collective capacity of governing in mutual interest and cooperation, not to mention our imagination as to who or what constitutes a person or population in need of care. Given the planetary scope of the pandemic, there must be other ways of organizing a response besides those based on the deeply fraught condition of "citizenship."

The virus migrated too. It had its own career, and few locations provided refuge from it. It moved in waves from "first-tier" to "second-tier" cities and into more rural areas. Along the way it drew its own map of human society. Many of us with family, friends, and colleagues in China stayed in close contact with them while the outbreak grew, and then watched in disbelief as our own countries sat on their hands, wallowing in an unjustified psychological distance from the rest of the world. It provided for a kind of Cassandra complex, of knowing exactly what was going to happen because you had seen it happen elsewhere at a distance, but could not convince people of what was coming their way. But the wave was real.

Foresight aside, in many places access to medical care is highly conditional. Even as populations continue the long historical arcs of intermingling, crisis responsibility for the care and supervision of any one person is retained by a state that may be on the other side of the world, and which can only provide care if that person returns to their birthing grounds. Even then, access is not certain. For other migrants, therefore, a forced return is what prevents access to care.

Alternatives exist to the artificial segmentation of the human population into discrete tracts of the planet's surface. Best-practice medical care can, in principle, be provided anywhere. In contrast with autochthonous fallacies, it is possible for humanity to be amalgamated and disentangled, gathered and dispersed, self-sorted and self-assembled based on all sorts of different spatial logics. As the license of "citizen" is simultaneously reinforced and undermined by contemporary geopolitics, and as other credentials assume its place, or multiply it, a range of possible post-pandemic positions is already being innovated, for better and worse.

The question is not a matter of whether the world should never be sorted, but how else it could be sorted in a way that is more viable because less punitive and restrictive. Given that cloud platforms can provide state-scale services regardless of location, and given that state services increasingly rely on the cloud, perhaps they too will come to be available beyond normal borders. On the other hand, not all migration is as voluntary or as coerced as the great pandemic filtering—not by far. The future of climate migration, for example, and what proactive and reactionary measures are taken to deal with it, threatens to be among the most fraught demographic issues of the century. Will policies that allow the migration toward or away from countries of passport bring about a foundational economy for states directly selling admission? As with Barbados, will the benefits of exit outweigh the costs, including the literal price of entrance?

The precedents and possibilities cut several ways. The mobilization toward a feasible "post-Anthropocene" world, conducted at the required planetary scale, will demand an extraordinary choreography, a broad and deep commitment to public and private reason, including unfamiliar forms of sacrifice and behavior change, a pragmatic vision for what is and is not "essential," and a focusing of technical systems on equity and efficiency. One upside of the big filtering and of the uneven mass mobilizations of the pandemic is that this seems perhaps more possible, even likely, compared to just a year ago.

For all these reasons, those who suspect the "plandemic" as a trial run for planetary governance of climate change–related emergencies are hopefully not wrong in every regard. Let us allow that in coming years the valence and connotations of the term "New World Order" will shift in interesting ways, more as a foundational geopolitical and geoeconomic realignment than as an elite conspiracy based on the symbology of "666."

As for how the Westphalian format of state "citizenship" is redesigned, the reorganization of geopolitics may include rights of exit *and* entrance, likely even in forms that are incompatible with one another. These may open some borders while multiplying others, fortifying historical public states and proliferating privatized urban fields, platforms, and networks. These may be admirable or not: an open planetary surface dotted with private enclaves, or, vice versa, a largely private surface with public enclaves, each with different conditions of membership. The inquiries on behalf of these and other geopolities are not *against governmentality*, but are on behalf of its reimagining—not the end of history, but something like a long-delayed next beginning.

3

COMPARATIVE GOVERNANCE

Having been filtered and sorted back into countries of passport, the global population participated in what future political science may look back upon as *the largest control experiment in comparative governance in history*, with the virus as the control variable and hundreds of different states and political cultures as the experimental variables. The results are plain to see.

How different jurisdictional models, political architectures, and political cultures responded to this pandemic is a kind of litmus test, a way to evaluate the effectiveness and logic of those systems and the cultures that animate them. And we see extremely different outcomes. Countries that took the situation and the data seriously, that had governments that were trusted and competent, that used technology directly and effectively, and that already had equitable and comprehensive health care systems did well. Those that did not, did not. In short, more is not always more: relative GDP was less of a factor than the quality of governance.

How different systems responded should affect how political cultures evaluate their traditions. Brazil is failing, Taiwan is succeeding, Iran was hit hard, Vietnam seems to have done well, India was helped somewhat by having a young population, many African countries managed well, Italy did poorly at first but then did better than the UK and other parts of Europe. The responses of Singapore and Texas could not have been more different. There are also clear differences between responses within the same country: between Hong Kong and Shanghai, Moscow and St. Petersburg, California and Arizona, and so on.

As of this writing, the story is far from over. We see that Germany did reasonably well because of widely available testing and therapeutic responses, at least at first, and then less well as time went on. Sweden had much higher numbers than its Scandinavian neighbors, but lower than might have been expected given that it never mandated a lockdown. This shows just how much a universally available health system providing excellent care gets you, and also how much more that would have helped in directly curtailing the contagion elsewhere.

The range of responses reveals much about the political capacity of those different systems and cultures. Some aspects of centralized command and control have worked, others have not. Some strengths of Western liberalism have worked in response to the virus, particularly at the edges, while other aspects have left their societies in a numb incoherent daze, mumbling rationalizations. Each system faces the same test at the same time. What lessons must be learned from this experiment, even if there is no one single criterion of success? Those who did worse should learn from, and seek in different ways to emulate, those that did better. It would be an even greater stupidity to overlook that opportunity.

To be sure, we must not take all reported data at face value, and testing for antibodies shows the first major strain of the virus is possibly much more widespread (and perhaps less lethal) than originally suspected, though the increases in reported deaths versus expected deaths (regardless of what "cause" is assigned) shows the total number of deaths is also probably much higher than generally reported. As of this writing, China reports about 90,000 cases and Russia 4.4 million, and most assume the real numbers are much higher. But even if we multiply the number of Chinese cases by a factor of 10 or 100, the United States' 30 million cases, Brazil's 11.5 million cases, and India's 11 million (all of which will go much higher) are indictments of the nationalist populist regimes that oversaw a catastrophe caused by multiple factors they couldn't reconcile with the petty, insular chauvinism on which their power depends.

What is the pattern? One, quite clearly, is that the populist "we will do what we like" school of thought did really poorly, whereas the more-prepared, technocratic countries with robust and widely available public health care and trust in governing responses did better by comparison, sometimes avoiding harm from both the virus and the blunt instrument of long-term lockdown. Good governance governs better.

Oxford University published what it called the "Comprehensive Government Response Tracker," which compared several variables regarding how states did and did not respond, and allows for some rough correlations between types of intervention and outcomes. However, there is more to the story. Political culture matters too. What may be acceptable in one place would have been rejected in another. Furthermore, every country's response did not start at the same time. China, obviously, was hit first, and its neighboring areas were next, though Taiwan, Singapore, South Korea, and Vietnam, for example, were able to react quickly, partially because of their experience with SARS in 2002. The United States and Europe had several weeks' warning of what was coming but were still caught largely off-guard.

The Trump administration, in particular, sat on its hands and waved away the oncoming contagion as an annoying interruption, then a conspiracy, then claimed victory regardless. The United States' congenitally isolationist mentality was a terrible weakness: it remained impervious even as millions sounded the alarm. Political cultures that emphasize a self-congratulatory aesthetics of liberal individualism are optimized for certain things and not for others. They are still quite capable of top-down, planned, coordinated action, as their militaries and game shows demonstrate.

By contrast, many Asian technocracies did well. This won't sit well with some across the political spectrum for different reasons, but it is true. Taiwan, off the coast of mainland China, has 22 million people and 984 cases *total*.

The city of San Diego, where I am in lockdown once again, is doing the best out of California's big cities and it is still reporting over 4,000 cases per day. Los Angeles does 4,000 before lunch. California, with the fifth-largest economy by GDP in the world and a governor who seemed to take the situation seriously, has reported over 3.5 million total cases. By contrast, Singapore has reported a pandemic total of 59,000, South Korea has had 92,000, and Vietnam only 2,562. Obviously, reporting in the last of these may not be as complete as with the former two, but time will tell with antibody testing. The numbers will continue to go up dramatically before this is over, but the relevant patterns will not.

Another important lesson is that it is misleading to attribute a country's success to a single approach, whether one based on a strong technological intervention of testing and tracking, or a robust health care system that acts on what is known, or a political culture in which people trust the information they are given and what they are told to do. All of these are critical; without any one in place, a society puts itself at risk, both epidemiological and economic.

Taiwan achieved its success without the kind of blanket lockdown seen in Wuhan or Washington. The country relied on early, quick, and pervasive testing and tracking, allowing for a more targeted and therapeutic quarantining of those at risk of causing or receiving contagion. It was able to keep schools and offices largely open. The authorities, including the digital minister, Audrey Tang, had an intelligent plan and were well coordinated. They had earned significant public trust over the past years. The messaging, reporting, and follow-through were credible. Compare this with how the lumbering, self-pitying United States and the United Kingdom plodded through, and how their confused policy responses left them vulnerable to maximum epidemiological and economic pain, akin to ripping the bandage off as slowly and gruesomely as possible.

When many of those in the West are presented with the reality of the Asian countries' effective response to the virus, the level of denial, ignorance, rationalization, self-deception, and paranoia is a sight to behold. Much of it is motivated by straight-up racism: "Asia can manage because the nature of the Oriental is despotic and robotic." "They don't care about privacy because life is cheap." "China can read my mind through AI." "They made COVID-19 on purpose!!!"

Lest anyone think I mean to present the "Asian technocratic" response in too warm a light, it is certainly the case that the Chinese numbers were achieved at costs that would be impossible elsewhere for good reason. Also, the early months of the pandemic will be remembered for propagandistic episodes of the *theater of authority and competence*, illustrated by images, such as men in hazmat suits spraying down streets with disinfectant in the rain, that represent less a calculated, objective response than a public show of proficient "intervention" for its own sake. The cause-versus-correlation dynamics of these kinds of stunts (and there were many such) and the apparent success in governing the pandemic should not be confused. You don't catch COVID-19 from the asphalt. Authoritarian performance art has no real potency, whether in the costume of command or strong-man indifference.

The clear lesson, probably to no one's surprise, is that nationalist populism is not a particularly effective approach to the governance of complex realities that are immune to the bluster of xenophobic myth-mongering. The numbers bear this out. The countries that did the worst in deaths per capita are piloted by the magical thinking of nationalist populism. By that measure, United Kingdom did by far the worst. Alongside them on this ignominious chart are Brazil, Mexico, Iran, Chile, Colombia, and of course the United States, all on parade demonstrating definitively what is *not* a viable planetary biopolitics.

Countries whose heads of state are not only untrustwor-thy, but whose very occupation of their office is dependent on a larger and deeper *political culture of suspicion of govern-ance*, policy, and expertise, enter into a self-fulfilling cycle by which the suspicion—well-founded or not—engenders forms of governance that are indeed dubious and manifest incompetence, which in turn reinforces suspicion in governance as such. The result of this experiment in comparative governance is not only about certain kinds of regimes, but also political cultures that, after setting the stage for themselves over years, make given policies vari-ously possible or unthinkable.

But regardless of who is in power, what are sometimes derisively called *historically ungovernable cultures* (again, looking at you, Texas, Brazil, Italy, etcetera) also did less well. As if by design, the cultures where governance itself is refused were also those that became much more difficult to in fact govern, making them hardest hit by the pandemic, such that a vicious circular dynamic ruled. The impossibility of governance ensures that the negative effects of the absence of effective governance are guaranteed, which in turn amplifies suspicion of the role of governance.

Still, the story of the populists is more complex than that. While their ascension may owe to valid or invalid distrust of secular elite expertise, economic precarity, sociocultural anomie, and so on, their power is not based solely on the withdrawal of state authority, but rather on the *personalization* of that authority into themselves and into the national meta-narrative they conjure, via a politics of performativity that incentivizes incredible mental gymnastics by its partisans.

With particular relevance for this or any biopolitical emergency, the assumption of authority back into the person of the ruler can be seen as a reversal of what Michel Foucault showed as the historical shift from *sovereign power*, whereby governing authority rested in the person of the monarch, to *biopower*, where it rested in the capacity of the state to structure the conditions of biological life and administer the health of a population through scientific categorization, normalization, therapeutics, and prediction. The anti-modernity platforms of today's pseudo-sovereigns, including suspicion of science, evolution, climate change, and genomics, on behalf of their post-secular superstitions, are *an abdication from modern biopolitics*. This abdication is built on the attempted assumption of sovereign power that sees the planet as a world subordinated to the insular mythos of distinct organic communities. The fact that, through the "big filtering," the sovereigns could capture their far-flung citizens and subject them to this sophistic bombast ensured that even those who know better could not escape their ineptitude. In this regard, their ability to wield a negative biopolitics rests upon claims of such sovereignty.

Trump pulled medical advice out of whatever obsequious cavity congratulated him most recently, Bolsonaro raved about the Marxist vegetarians who are too effeminate to withstand the viral incursion into their bodies, Modi pointed the finger at Muslims who may have planned this all along, and Boris Johnson muttered about Churchill something something. Others seethed at Big Pharma. Russia's intense mix of scientific heritage and esoteric medievalism, its closed linguistic and narrative universe, acknowledged the reality of the virus in the abstract, including rushing a vaccine by moving the goalposts of trial testing. Meanwhile, Lukashenko, still the president of Belarus (as of this writing), said the virus simply doesn't exist, and according to the logic of personalized sovereignty, if he says it doesn't then it doesn't.

They all failed in similar ways, while the virus continued unabated. They managed to cosplay the magical will of authority and to defer and delay the work of the pinhead experts with their damn statistics, but in the face of an indifferent virus spreading through the animal bodies of their constituents, reality has the last word. This is so because beyond mobilizing a congregation to all think the same thing for a little while, performative politics doesn't actually *work* as a way of deciding life and death. The world is not, finally, a text.

For the Western (and Eurasian) authoritarian populists, their postmodernism is mobilized for a premodern politics and ends up constructing a very different kind of authoritarianism than the Asian technocratic sort. It is an authoritarian anarchism: a warlordism that makes use of the remaining machinery of liberal secular states to maintain the semblance of economic order.

The moment when people's lives and livelihoods are put at risk by the *excruciatingly loud void* that could have been filled by a rational, competent, comprehensive, coordinated governance should imply the end of empty symbolism taking the place of proper policy. Will it be the end? The tenacity of self-defeating populism is fierce. We see it in the "the revenge against the revenge of the real" in mask wars and anti-vaccine politics, and in the overlap of technophobia and xenophobia. Our human ability to bend facts to favor narratives remains steadfast.

The clear conclusion of this comparison of governance points away from zombie sovereign power and toward a *positive biopolitics at planetary scale*. We can glimpse a bit of what that positive biopolitics may look like in what did work well. First, the culture of data matters. Cities and national and governments that had well-structured data platforms and were able to sense relevant information, bring it to the fore, communicate in a credible and consistent way were able to get greater social buy-in for what would later become more ambitious forms of focused intervention. In countries that were less successful in this regard, where people had less trust in the veracity of the data, or why data matters at all, it became increasingly impossible to coordinate proper responses, leaving them with the worst combination of draconian and anarchic improvisations.

Second, at least for the West, the generational dismantling of public governance, beginning in the neoliberal era, accelerating with the recent populist wave and the deliberate staffing of institutions with incompetents, has left wealthy societies comically helpless. Whether justified by an idea that free-floating finance is all that is necessary to steer a society, or that bottom-up elective communities and networks of self-organizations can immediately do everything states once did but without the insults of hierarchy, the notion that complex systems such as human societies can do without top-down steerage finds its limit.

Third, the aesthetic dichotomy between technological and social institutional responses is fictitious. The best responses were based on both. It is necessary for a society to be able to sense, model, and act back upon itself, and it is necessary for it to plan and provide for the care of its people. The retort that technical interventions, such as patched-together tracing apps, are facile "solutionism," deployed in panic because proper planning and care are not there to enable more targeted approaches, has much more than a grain of truth to it, even when it comes from those who wrongly reject the role of sensing, modeling, tracing, and calculations as anything other than invasive or repressive.

The implication of this experiment in comparative governance is that a positive and planetary-scale biopolitics is not only necessary, it is also possible. One of the core cultural foundations of that post-pandemic politics is something we all have learned more than a bit about: the *epidemiological view of society*.

4

THE EPIDEMIOLOGICAL
VIEW OF SOCIETY

Toward that positive biopolitics, we can see how quickly people learned to see society as epidemiology does, not as self-contained individuals entering into contractual relationships, but as a population of contagion nodes and vectors. That our common biological circumstance means we help or harm one another by simply coming in contact is a fact that precedes, and in principle should override, other subjective cultural divisions and associations. With COVID-19, viral contagion is dangerous, but the risk is not just individual. It is a collective risk. Dashboard interfaces and statistical models of contagion have become the visual profile of the event. The image of our interconnected whole seen in these reflections should stay with us, long after data fatigue and the immediate crisis pass.

The epidemiological view should shift our sense of subjectivity away from private individuation and toward public transmissibility. Emphasis shifts from personal experience and toward responsibilities couched in the underlying biological and chemical realities that bind us. The dynamic between the individual and society broadens and connects with the enmeshed whole through which each of us lives. Each organism is a transmission medium for information—from ideas to viruses—and is defined by who and what each is connected to and disconnected from. The political premise of "immunization"—to make oneself immune by excluding someone or someone else—must be couched in conceptual and technical models of the social that are as inclusive and agnostic as epidemiological models and which carry the same weight of shared responsibility. This means a likely change in how we see relationships between individuals and the whole of society, and in self-identification and symbolic interaction. For some this is an affront to identity and for others its precondition.

This epidemiological model of society is foundational for a viable post-pandemic politics. It is the basis for rethinking our role and position in society and even what a society is. Habits of thought need reform. Here subjectivity is not conceived in the common sense of a self-sovereign individual that subsequently enters into social and economic relationships, nor as part of a collective given shape by its allegiance to a set of symbolic obligations. Both of these give way instead to an appreciation of the social that is more biological, even biochemical.

"Risk" rather than being understood as a private algebraic decision, it is defined from the start as a plural and intersubjective set of relations. The individual may be a risk to the collective, if they are contagious, or in turn may be at risk from the collective, in which case they are to be protected. At the same time, the immunological principle of vaccination is one in which herd immunity reduces the individual's risk and, in turn, the individual's own immunity contributes to that achievement. The pandemic has made it easier to see oneself more as a node in a biopolitical network to which one is responsible than as an autonomous individual whose sovereignty is guaranteed by free will or in the image of the national autocrat's symbolic prestige, at least for most people.

This is a big change. It should be secured. This political epistemology of the species works against the folk image of the somatic body, cleansed of external contaminants, and presumes instead a biological economy of symbiotes, inside of us and us inside of them. For this the coronavirus are recognized less through the simple trope of the "invader" and more as a specific entity against which our species decides to define its own always-uncertain immunological borders. It arrives not from "the outside," but is recognized as being long co-present with us. Through the deliberate and artificial behavioral and medical interventions of masks, antibody testing, and eventually vaccines, as we *change ourselves* to resist its viral RNA, it is neutralized, not annihilated.

This is part of a post-pandemic biopolitics that is *evolutionary* in the most materialist and cooperative sense of the dynamic and directable unfolding of life. Through the lens of this biological materialism, the conception of oneself becomes less an interiority occupied by private voice and experience and more a medium through which the physical world signifies itself. The reflection may look counterintuitive in the mirror, but it hits home in the allocentric mapping of self-in-the-world provided by the epidemiological statistical models and charts of the pandemic that we all inhabit.

Foucault's 1977–78 lectures at Collège de France, published in English as *Security, Territory, Population*, outline the European beginnings of modern epidemiological politics with the organization of the response to smallpox. It is here that his theory of biopower is established as "the specific strategies of power which developed through an understanding of humans as a species," founded on empirical science, predictive statistical models, and the deliberate and prescriptive "normalizing" toward a model ideal, in this case, to induce bodies to conform to the norm of not having or spreading smallpox. Smallpox vaccination is particularly interesting because, for the first time, "statistical instruments and the certain and generally applicable character of vaccination and variolization made it possible to think of the phenomena in terms of the calculus of probabilities."

He identifies four innovative disciplinary foundations to modern medical governance: the *case*, to measure and predict the path of contagion; the *risk*, to predict who is most at risk; the *danger*, to identify the variable that will mitigate risk, including mandatory vaccination and the spatial controls of quarantine (such as healthy living quarters, regulations for public buildings, quarantine procedures); and the *crisis*, to model and understanding the spiking and flattening arcs of infection over time. In different forms, these remain the essential methodologies today. They rely on preventative medicine, including the achievement of herd immunity through planned distribution of vaccinations, whereas previous interventions sought to suppress the disease by preventing direct contact between those infected and those who were not. In contrast, interventions utilizing vaccination and variolization conceptualized the sick and healthy people as a whole, and then modeled a probable morbidity given the groups and circumstances to which particular individuals belonged.

As Foucault outlines, this epidemiological mode shifts the final authority from the declaration of the sovereign to the expert administration of life and death, now credentialized by a quite different and more secular authority. For COVID-19, a positive biopolitics competed with, on the one hand, a populist return to sovereign power, and on the other, the weight of a *negative* biopolitics. Put simply, this negative biopolitics reads the history of the biopower of modern epidemiological intervention as an oppressive hierarchical and normalizing discursive–technical apparatus that should be relentlessly critiqued and not actively resisted. "Insubordination" against the state and its power/knowledge is both the project and the plan, and the exploration of living differently takes precedence, perhaps even over preventable deaths.

The orthodox interpretation of the significance of Foucault is not (usually) on behalf of a "return" to sovereign power, but on behalf of a ceaseless interrogation of biopower itself. It entails a definition of power and, by extension of biology, as a differential field of relations that produces modes of subjectivity through material–discursive institutionalization, such that the real political target should be the hierarchical and normalizing effects of power *as such*. As power relations are detected, then they are subjected to critical dismantling (rather than being seen as, for example, the technical division of labor in a complex society). This has inspired or informed some of the most influential scholarship in the Humanities for almost half a century.

This tendency has also led to a debilitating and lazy constructivism for which the cultural contingencies that, for example, framed how human bodies were interpreted in early modern European medicine have been less demystified than elevated to a first principle of social epistemology. Reality recedes further and further away as the insistence that it is all discourse extends all the way down. It is here that the orthodox biopolitical critique is, unfortunately, aligned with the populist Right. Each attacks the ability of society to sense, model, and act back upon itself in terms of biological assemblage according to the best available information. At their extremes, both valorize political performativity over scientific empiricism, both eschew the very notion of objectivity, and both are crippled by self-paralyzing magical thinking. One sees positive biopolitics as an unnatural usurpation of the dignity and tradition of pre-Darwinian cosmologies, disrupting natural social hierarchies, while the other sees it as the imposition of a quantitative and positivist fundamentalism, reinforcing artificial social hierarchies. Despite their conflicts, sometimes they collaborate directly, sometimes they show up for the same rallies, and sometimes they are not even aware of overlapping. Meanwhile, the virus does its thing.

The most extremist visions of such negative biopolitics are offered by philosophers such as Giorgio Agamben, who put it as such when (literally) comparing airport security to the management of Auschwitz: "The relation between individuals and the state involves the routine inscription and registration of the most private and most *incommunicable element of subjectivity*, the biopolitical life of the body" (emphasis mine). I will consider Agamben's responses to the pandemic in some detail in the following chapters, but here already we see the heart of the matter. In truth, the biopolitical life of the body is not private, not incommunicable, and not subjective in the sense he means. It is public, communicable, and intersubjective. This is the basis of epidemiology.

Against his theological–phenomenological preferences, a positive biopolitics must embrace a realist and materialist conception of the human body as a biochemical assemblage and collective human intelligence as the collaboration of such creatures working in concert. That collaboration is based on movements between inside and outside, multiple levels of nested parasitism and symbiosis, viral life, and the composting stew of interdependence. The "collectivity" of intelligence comes from how we grasp these processes through technical abstraction. This allows a particular sapient species, that is us, not only to be part of that condition but to conceptualize it and to act back upon it deliberately.

Positive biopolitics is the rationalism of the living, not the dead. It is a political and philosophical commitment to the real against reactionary constructivism and traditionalist vitalism. The notion that life is just too mysterious to grasp or that the natural order is too sacred to fiddle with, and that this actually suffices as the basis of an effective and ethical medical policy, is the daydream of a comfortable class who does not live with the daily agencies of sewage landscapes and exposed corpses.

5
THE SENSING LAYER

The epidemiological model of society is dependent on knowing what is really happening. Collective self-composition needs to sense the world in order to make valid models of it. Just as with animal organisms, thinking cannot really be physically separated from sensing and sensation. At the level of the city and an entire health system, sensing is also a layer in a biopolitical "stack" of different technologies, institutions, and behaviors.

During the pandemic, testing and tracing were key aspects of the "sensing layer" of the governing epidemiological models. Without them the models are guesswork, but do we see them this way? Infomercials for "smart cities" have taught us to think of "sensors" only as exotic, expensive chips, and some notions of social politics to think of public health only in terms of non-technological therapeutic care. Each misses a significant part of the picture.

Ultimately, testing and sensing are the same thing. To have more widely available testing is to have more accurate sensing, which means better models, which means a better public health response. To have inadequate planning and provision for testing is to have inadequate modeling, which means inadequate governance. Cities that have passed this test are the ones that have flattened the curve effectively. Cities that have failed the test are turning sports arenas into makeshift morgues.

And so, a good definition of the sensing layer refers to all of the ways in which a society is able to sense what is going on at both granular and holistic levels so as to make a model that it may use to act back upon itself and thereby govern itself. The principle applies to more than the pandemic. Climate science produces models of the planet based on atmospheric sensors, surface-level sensors, all manner of on-site thermometers and monitors, archives of ice core samples, and so on, each of which produces little bits of information that then contribute to models of change abstracted from the sum of individual moments of sensing.

In the context of the pandemic, the sensing layer includes access to testing, to diagnosis, and to being a body that *counts*. To be excluded from testing and being sensed is to not count. Again, advanced technical means of sensing are not the opposite of equitable and effective direct care; the two depend on each other to work. The aesthetic dichotomy between high-tech and high-touch forms of sensing cannot hold.

The sensing layer is made up of many different kinds of technologies, different kinds of encounters. Some of them may be quite intimate, some quite visceral, some quite distantiated, some non-tactile, some immediate, some highly mediated, but all contribute to the aggregate model of the human under care.

When nurses risk their own health to welcome strangers into the clinic, insert a metal tube into their veins, withdraw their blood, and prepare it for testing, that is the sensing layer. When a frontline worker holds an infrared scanner to another stranger's forehead and logs their current body temperature, that is the sensing layer.

When a city builds a medical testing facility capable of processing samples fast enough that the person represented by the sample knows if they are well or not, that is the sensing layer. When test kits are not available and the clinic uses an MRI to detect damage to a patient's lungs as a way of telling her she likely did have the virus, that is also the sensing layer. When all these are available to anyone who may be vulnerable, that, too, is the sensing layer. When those most vulnerable to comorbidities are identified and protected, and when reporting protocols are transparent, accurate, and trustworthy, that is the sensing layer. When any or all of them are failed or broken, that is a broken sensing layer, and that society is in the dark.

All of these forms of sensing are done in the service of a *model abstraction*, which concerns not just statistics but social relations. For the epidemiological model of society, one body counts and is included in the same aggregate model through which another body is given care. This only works because the collective aggregation produces a more accurate picture of the whole that is *not* what we experience by dead reckoning. You cannot see a virus. The model is a collective intelligence about something that is true even though it can never be personally experienced.

For all this, there is a composition, a choreography, and a coordination of these disparate moments into a whole. At the same time, that model doesn't exist without these fleeting moments by which the world senses itself, and those moments don't have the function and profile we ask of them without being aggregated into an abstraction greater than themselves. For this data is more produced than "extracted." That is, although the virus and the underlying biological reality are real, the data is artificial; it is an instance produced by sensing rather than an already constituted entity to be plucked. Choices are necessary to structure what the layer may or may not see, and the contours of inclusion are variable and produce different models and so different governances. Such a model is a picture not only of what it discloses about the world, but also of the circumstances of its own construction.

Therefore, inclusion also implies exclusion. The implication of this applies not only to "big data" but to all the ways we sense each other, and all the intimacies at a distance that are part of how we compose ourselves as a society. It extends to recognizing instances where medical care is unequally and inappropriately distributed, overprovided to the wealthy and old at the expense of the poor and young. The permanently shifting question of how we provide for ourselves is answered in patterns of relative access and exclusion. But as far as the model is concerned, exclusion also means occlusion: those uncounted are also unseen.

Balancing requirements that everyone is seen but only in the right way is extremely difficult. Forms of observation that may be colloquially recognized as "surveillance" (such as antibody tests and temperature checks) are also the very means by which people have secured the right to be counted and accounted for: the *right* to be tested, measured, modeled. Post-pandemic politics needs to think through these relationships carefully and with the goal that the whole of society is included in the model appropriately. Errors cut in several directions. As I will discuss, the demand to protect the illusion of individual autonomy by refusing the responsibilities relating to co-immunity claims the mantle of bioethics in bad faith.

The shape of the pandemic as a social fact is outlined in the global social mobilization around the virus as a governing variable, and in the distorted structure of access, vulnerability, and responsibility at individual, urban, and planetary scales. And so what the sensing layer is sensing is not just the presence of a virus but movement across the uneven surfaces of global society. It senses us as we are and are not. In the blind spots, the virus also senses all the ways we have neglected ourselves and one another.

An outcome of that biopolitics is the irrationally distorted provision of testing and care, which makes the sensing layer less able to produce a coherent model of the collective risk, which in turn amplifies the risk, which then in turn makes the absence of a viable model more dangerous. By contrast, the architecture of a positive biopolitical governance that is broadly responsive to the whole, regardless of individual position, would be the basis not only of how one participates in the biopolitical constituency, but also of the way that planetary society is constituted by that participation and by the ubiquity and universality of its services.

The sensing layer is a means for societal self-understanding, but, in concert with the models it can produce and the institutional enforcement of its implications, it is also a kind of instantiation of a collective immune system. That is, for the longer term, we need to think of the sensing layer as part of a larger epidemiological and biopolitical stack in the service of a collective formation, a means by which society not only senses and simulates itself, but also constructs itself.

6

MODEL SIMULATIONS

The epidemiological view of society shifts our sense of subjectivity from one that is internalized toward one that is externalized into, for example, model simulations. Such models function best for post-pandemic politics when they turn that externalization into a medium of collective self-composition. Good governance without good models is extraordinarily difficult; it leads to blunt, low-resolution responses, such as blanket lockdowns, instead of targeted interventions.

A society may only act upon itself based on the information it has and heeds. During the pandemic, the most successful societies used their sensing layer to produce and share multiple models of the changing situation and used these as a medium of action. Others, not having robust models, or ignoring them or distorting them, saw deadly neglect, resulting from either paralysis or deliberate inaction on behalf of a politics of sovereign myth and short-term self-interest.

Think back to the earlier weeks and months of the pandemic and all the time spent staring at the charts and graphs and figures and diagrams on your screen, searching for a clue as to what was happening and what might happen next. To cope, we became amateur epidemiologists and learned to see ourselves accordingly. In gauging how close the wolf was to the door by reading graphs, we learned a new representation of the social, and so learned a new way to conceptualize what the social is. That way of seeing is something that will remain with us.

We learn many different ways of orienting ourselves in the world, from touch and balance to satellite tracking. Each informs a different kind of interface culture. Some interfaces, such as map apps, show "you" from the outside, and these allocentric orientations demand literacy with quantitative and diagrammatic abstractions and a strategic ability to locate oneself within them. Other interfaces, such as first-person video games, orient the world around the perceptual point of the viewer and compress the whole world into a tunnel-vision of egocentric navigation whereby everything is shown as an ever-expanding stream from nowhere, just for you.

How you see yourself depends on how you see the world, and during a pandemic the world is epidemiological, outlined by specific visual vernaculars of what constitutes risk, pattern, curve, prediction, and recommendation. For this, there is always a figure–ground perception at work. Seeing ourselves in essence as the *ground* for which this virus is the *figure* trains us to imagine society as a confluence of interlocking and cascading causes and effects, at once impersonal and tactile. The afterimages of these models become part of a public literacy through which we grasp the situation viscerally and locate ourselves in an immunological commons. This retraining will persist after the crisis.

For post-pandemic politics, social models must be accurate and effective to be reliable: they must be valid representations of the underlying reality, which depends on the presence of an inclusive sensing layer, but for them to also work as a medium for societal self-composition, the models must not just reflect reality; they also need to be able to change it. Models are not only a means by which we learn to see ourselves within an epidemiological whole, but are increasingly the means through which society self-composes. They are the essential social technology of positive biopolitics.

The granularity of the model, how accurate it is down to the smallest unit, is important, but not because that positive biopolitics demands omniscience. Omniscience doesn't matter as much as heuristics: Will this work? Is this model modeling what really matters? Will this have the intended effect? A perfect simulation of the world that cannot act upon the world is not a medium of governance; it is a game. That said, low-resolution and low-confidence models (as well as health care systems inadequately prepared by design) are what made the crude instrument of broad lockdown more necessary than it might have been otherwise. While it is true that "numbers do not bleed; people do," it's also true that with lousy numbers, there will be more bleeding.

The architecture of a viable post-pandemic biopolitics therefore depends upon the scope, validity, and appropriateness of the data, all dependent on a sensing layer that has been well composed and which is able to enforce the implications of its models. So, what is the problem? It is not for lack of technological know-how or capacity. Instead, we have been using the technologies upon which such models depend for far less important things (advertising, arguing, the monetization of affectation, etc.), especially during the recent years of the surge of populist politics. Perhaps the use of these technologies in this way and the populist surge are even the same thing, as a false sense of subjectivity is constructed, curtailed, and amplified through the hyper-reductive format of the self-reinforcing individual user feed.

In other words, the possibility of using these technologies for a positive biopolitics is prevented by the structuring demands of myopic capital drawing upon political and interface cultures of *hyperindividuation*. The problem is less with quantitative modeling itself than with what else we have asked it to do and why. That can and must change. But for that to happen, especially in the West, there needs to be a shift in the cultural valence of sensing and what is called "surveillance."

7
SURVEILLANCE IS NOT
THE RIGHT WORD

One of the most difficult challenges of governing responses to the pandemic has been the development and deployment of infection tracing and tracking platforms, which may include not just apps on phones, but tens of thousands of social workers checking and reconstructing infection vectors and enforcing quarantines face-to-face and hour-by-hour. Generally, in the West these efforts have been both chaotic and contentious. This is not the case everywhere. Having gone through SARS-2, Taiwan had a system prepared, and was able to do effective tracing through a combination of high-tech and high-touch, and to support quarantine efforts simply through cell tower triangulation. This required coordination and compliance that may be culturally impossible and thus politically impossible in other countries.

The controversies about tracing in many Western

countries were based on concerns that private platforms would use the cover of the emergency to get their claws deeper into the private worlds of their users. This led to both serious debates on who should be building the digital means of production and unserious shouting matches based on rumor and insinuation. The sad story of the United Kingdom's bungling attempts to build and deploy an app for this purpose is a minor scandal in itself. In the United States, Google and Apple, makers of the two most used mobile operating systems, collaborated on a contagion tracer app based on encrypted Bluetooth signals, but the federal response and fifty state responses were each so "sovereign" that, as of this writing, it was not even possible to get caseloads to a level where coordinated app-assisted contact tracing could help. The system never got itself together enough for the app to be useful. Post–General Data Protection Regulation expectations as to the dynamics between American cloud platforms and European tech sovereignty were scrambled when Google and Apple refused various European government requests to make their app *less* anonymous because that would expose their users to privacy vulnerabilities.

Here the trade-off is not just between a system that works well as an epidemiological technology and one that a public will actually download and use. In this case, we also observe a disconnect between legitimate if costly suspicions, concerns, and refusals concerning how the technology actually works and those concerning how people *imagine* the technology must work. The latter, based on thematically consistent if also untrue misconceptions, are often supported by both mainstream and fringe media: the tracing apps are directly linked to your email account, or passport, or they use your phone's camera somehow, or they add your name to a special permanent government database, etc. Add this to the real underlying chaos of the rollouts, and no wonder people are unenthusiastic. The dizzying variety of tracing apps in use throughout the world would make it impossible for anyone but the most dedicated tracker of trackers to have a clear picture.

Nevertheless, when public perception is based on cultivated paranoia, the hypothetical becomes the actual. Policy follows. To be sure, if the public debate orbits around not the merits and flaws of actually existing technologies but their mythological alter egos, then the result is that there isn't enough direct and open interrogation of the actual technologies as they are, and the public is left to argue with bogeymen.

Among these tall tales are not only domestic scenarios but also fantastically misinformed references to how similar approaches have been used in, specifically, Asian countries. In the West, lessons of the comparative governance and how responses were realized in countries like China, Taiwan, Singapore, and Vietnam are also being viewed through a distorted lens. The insistent tropes that the virus itself is "Chinese," that it may have been grown deliberately in a Chinese biotech laboratory, that it may have something to do with 5G, that it demands that we wear hazmat suits from a sci-fi movie, that "in China" the government responses are as dystopian and inhumane as you can dream up, and so on, are not confined to the fringes of Western biopolitical discourse. They are close to the center. "China" serves as the cautionary tale, but of what? For its part, Chinese state media has constructed its own wall of propagandistic nonsense, congratulating itself and blaming everyone else.

In the West, China is now so deeply associated with technology that *anxieties about technology are projected into anxieties about China*, and to an extent vice versa. Old Orientalist notions offer fake legibility and comfort for a Western dreamworld where the flipside of Sinofuturist fantasies is that fear of technology becomes fear of Asia. The hardcore version of the narrative is the evolution of the old "yellow horde" into new waves of emotionless robots. Add a genuinely psychologically destabilizing event like the pandemic, and the disturbances of a clear sense of agency and subjectivity in relation to epidemiological demands, and this outcome is not incomprehensible.

Such misapprehensions should be rejected by post-pandemic politics, even if the prospective demands for a positive biopolitics are not without controversy, legitimate and otherwise. The negative biopolitics is based on a too-common sense that all forms of society-scale sensing, modeling, and governance are, in essence, forms of pernicious "surveillance" and so should be resisted on those terms. Concurrent libertarian positions are based on the idea that individuals exist first in a state of self-sovereign freedom and are only later "captured" by technology or collective representation. Many responses, however, are based in wholly appropriate critiques of large private platforms whose manipulated models of society present it as composed merely and solely of hyperindividuated user profiles and predictions of their next desire, click, vote, or purchase.

While libertarian attitudes may be at home in different pockets among both the political Left and Right, they are antithetical to the epidemiological model of society that operates not at the level of individuals but of what connects them together. It is unlikely that the equitable and effective biopolitics that is needed for post-pandemic politics can emerge if wide-scale sensing and modeling is dismissed and resisted entirely as unwarranted "social control." The overinflation of the term "surveillance" is both politically debilitating and intellectually dishonest.

The pandemic has very likely changed some of the ways that we define, interpret, discuss, deploy, and resist sensing and modeling. Perhaps not. As the virus first reached Europe, another theorist of technology, based in Germany, argued to me that people should resist being tested for the virus and contributing to epidemiological models, because acquiescing to this regime would in the long run only encourage the invasive normalization of "big data biopolitics," which he went on to claim is, ultimately, inseparable from eugenics, the colonial-era slave trade, AI bias and the torture of Uighurs. He proudly said that he even told his students that they should all *refuse testing* and, having recently checked in on him, he maintains this position still.

In previous years he had a bigger audience for this line of thought, but fewer would see it his way now. Many are recognizing not that "surveillance is actually good," but rather that the suppressed positive potential of the technologies on which it depends demands attention and overdue realization. We could be using these technologies for much more important things than, for example, racial profiling and modeling individual consumers so as to predict which video they're likely to click on next. For post-pandemic biopolitics, the more necessary functions of planetary-scale computation that have been ignored or suppressed or sidelined come to the fore once again.

The epidemiological view of society and the agency of model simulations is changing the conversation about these matters. The debate isn't made easier by pandemics, but it is opened up in important ways. It is a mistake to reflexively interpret all forms of sensing and modeling as "surveillance" and all forms of active governance as punitive constraint. We need a different and more nuanced vocabulary.

In addition to the right to reasonable privacy there is also a right and responsibility to be counted. For post-pandemic biopolitics, inclusivity is essential. As said, equitable systems depend on the accuracy of models because the risk is always collective. However, as current controversies over citizenship and the census reveal, we see that certain neighborhoods, certain populations, certain types of inhabitants, certain less visible persons, places, and processes are undercounted, under-measured, under-accounted for, even unnamed, and are functionally invisible in terms of what is due to them.

To address this honestly, it is worth asking questions about the critical discourse of "anti-surveillance." At times it would appear that the term "surveillance" has ascended to the status of an almost sacred *negative concept* not only for libertarian-anarchist idealists but also for Western political culture in general, across the political spectrum, including the complacent center. It can function as a tenet around which entire worldviews of technology, globalism, urban planning, and the fictive autonomy of self-identity are made to orbit. Notions of "resistance" to surveillance, at once both fuzzy and axiomatic, credentialize entire art biennials, software movements, streaming documentaries, and political parties, and I am actually sympathetic to the bigger goals of many of these. But when the master concept is inflated and amplified to *explain* so very much about what's what and why, it is inevitable that the surveillance bubble will soon pop as more precise concepts appear to make sense of sensing, modeling, and prediction as a social technology.

An old joke might apply here: in the West, as a teenager you read either *Nineteen Eighty-Four* or *Atlas Shrugged*, and your politics are thereby cemented. Both of these works are Cold War novels about a self-sovereign individual who regains his stolen agency at the expense of the unwanted observation and interference from the larger social Other. Freedom means freedom from supervision, and so the heroic individual resists the oppressive and pervasive societal manipulation, finally realizing his solitary existential triumph. The themes are ingrained and built into the grammar of Western political common sense across the ideological spectrum. No wonder that when the United States built planetary-scale sensing and modeling infrastructures, its script for how they would be designed and received was so clear.

If we were to add to this list the one Foucault book for with which every undergraduate claims familiarity, *Surveiller et Punir / Discipline and Punish*, then philosophy's specific contribution to this tale becomes more clear. An intricately told history of the formation of the prone subject position of the prisoner as object of carceral logistics has devolved over successive retellings into the infamous meme: "factories are like prisons! schools are like prisons! prisons are like prisons!" To be sure, postpandemic biopolitics must include, not exclude, people whose public persona is based on their deep concern about algorithmic bias (quite real) but who nevertheless cannot name a single algorithm (A* search algorithm? Fast Fourier transform? Gradient descent?). When they don't really know what an algorithm is, but they are willing to take to the streets to demand that it be "fucked," then even if their instincts are not entirely wrong, the discourses available are failing them.

Like any such big vague idea, "anti-surveillance" falls under the diminishing returns of degradation into ever-increasingly dull-edged beliefs. A pro forma sterility of the critique becomes arduous and demoralizing. Handwringing op-eds "about what technology is doing to us," simultaneously po-faced and hysterical, obsessive and ignorant, radical and reactionary, echo a tedious and incredulous moralizing about contemporary digital etiquette. These are fixated less on weighing cumulative outcomes than on ensuring that one is not personally complicit with remote evils, based on self-evidently shoddy ideas about how relays of transitive harm between the moment of data capture and subsequent uses actually work. It is a politics of resentment oriented on the propriety of personal identity convened by what Polish writer Bogna Konior calls the "Anglo-Saxon luddite aristocracy." Another project is possible.

Exchanging manipulated attention capital for infrastructural access is not even remotely an ideal way to organize computation for a planetary society. But as the pandemic has very clearly demonstrated, robust and inclusive models are how any capable society comes to comprehend itself and compose itself. For a post-pandemic biopolitics, the circular reasoning and vicious cycle of "surveillance vs. anti-surveillance" frameworks must be replaced by a more polychromatic vocabulary so that a very different means of modeling production can be realized.

8

WHAT 5G STANDS FOR

Any prospective conception of post-pandemic politics must take into account what has gone so terribly wrong with pandemic politics, not only at official governmental levels but among the general public. From 5G conspiracy theories to mask protests to self-destructive super-spreader events that keep the economy on lockdown, the disconnect between rational policy and what people think and do is dangerously pronounced. This disconnect won't go away all by itself once the virus runs its course. It is not just exemplary of the *annus horribilis* of 2020, it is inseparable from the Western response to the pandemic and the realities that it makes clear. In relation to the fraught politics of surveillance, the intricate question of what should be the appropriate structures of planetary-scale sensing and computation, as opposed to its current one, presents itself under the shadow of conspiracy theory as the default mode of folk politics.

The problem is not just a few crazies. The number of people who you know that will refuse or have refused to get vaccinated for utterly spurious reasons will surprise you, if not shock you. What is going on? Belief in conspiracy theories is driven by several interlocking motives: *epistemic* (one's understanding of what is going on), *existential* (feelings of being safe and in control), and *social* (maintenance of a positive image of oneself and social group). These are all quite reasonable things to expect people to attempt to secure, but the rift between reality and subjective affirmation means one or the other has to give.

I suggest the real problem is not with the disclosures of the real and what they imply about how the world works, but that people are persecuted by those demands of self-affirmation. Again, the human world is an epidemiological and informational entanglement; we need to *stop making people crazy* with the demand for total individual autonomy, and stop conflating individuality with subjectivity, subjectivity with identity, and identity with agency so thoroughly that a challenge to one is a challenge to all. It is literally insane. No one can handle it.

The pandemic politics will be remembered for, among other things, the 5G conspiracy theories that tied the contagion to the installation of transmitters for millimeter wave cellular networks. The theories and their responses included dark references to tests in Wuhan, burning cell towers, pseudoscientific rumors about tumors, harassment of maintenance workers, celebrity tweets "just asking" leading questions, and eventually a fluid overlap and convergence with other modes of reactionary epidemiological biopolitics of the anti-vaccine and anti-mask movements.

This is the "nocebo effect" in full bloom. Reminiscent

of fears about photography absorbing the souls of its subjects, the general brooding sense that our identities are being "stolen" through the acceleration of "the system" links 5G's *yet faster* bandwidth for ego-corrosive social media to the de-subjectifying demands of pandemic public policy, driving some people to crack. For a few in the avant-garde, a vaccine logically therefore includes a "chip" that would ultimately invade and colonize one's biological person, dissolving its fragile integrity into an intolerable agglomerated capture.

The line between the rational and irrational is real but sometimes fuzzy. If Whole Foods Market exploits this uncertainty to sell "chemical-free water," the populist Right cynically encourages the political weaponization of symptomatic paranoid schizophrenia as a mass mobilization strategy. The overlap of conspiracy theory and anti-surveillance stories extends back further than *The Crying of Lot 49*, *Dr. Strangelove*, Victor Tausk and "the Influencing Machine," or Illuminati panics. The two are intertwined at the root. What is perhaps more unprecedented today is the rapid and ongoing regularization of these ideas into a global folk politics with real and ugly consequences. Just ask the US Capitol police.

Early in the pandemic, this deranged social movement staged massive anti-lockdown protest events in London and Berlin, where a cacophonous menagerie—libertarians, anti-vaccine celebrities such as Robert Kennedy Jr., Steve Bannon troops, actual Nazis, New Age yoga instructors, anarchists, "health freedom" advocates, conspiracy theorists in the mold of David Icke and Piers Corbyn, and possibly some of your friends and acquaintances—together found common cause. What is that cause? It is a self-amplifying *refusal of secular biopolitics*. For many that means also a defense of the populist Right leaders' attempts to revive sovereign power over insubordinate molecules and viral organisms, but for all it entails a radical social constructivism in which various fictive subjectivities (the nation, the individual, personal freedom, mystical intuition, etc.) refuse to acquiesce to the reality in which they are embedded because it is not how they wish to perceive it, even if those wishes are expressed through an allegiance to anxieties.

Their fear is palpable. The social and existential motivations for this symptomatic strain of pandemic political culture can be at least partially attributed to the genuine weirdness of the experience of the pandemic, and for sure, the ways that the epidemiological view of society and the political logics of secular biopolitics make many other claims on the real frighteningly irrelevant. It is scary for everyone but especially so for them.

Linking these misapprehensions, we see a pattern of imagined withdrawal from a world that is contaminated by technological mediation, and that is, for them, totalitarian *in the wrong way*. They are certain that the world is now attempting to introduce fatal harm to their bodies because it has already harmed their sense of agency and identity. The radicalization of interior counter-narrativizations that offer epistemic, existential, and social comfort is fortified by radical fantasy, maintained against mere "evidence": their deeper politics is to remain militantly loyal to a worldview undermined by epidemiological realism.

The ultimate claim of this cornered position is not just that their particular subjective sense of the world is the best, but that the sovereignty of individual subjectivity itself should decide what is true and real because it is *intrinsically valid*. It is a demand less on behalf of this or that specific belief; it is a resistance on behalf of *beliefs themselves* as opposed to a world in which each of us is— terrifyingly—"merely" biological. This is what draws that odd coalition into one. They are those for whom the Copernican revolution is stalled.

To be sure, the intense conflation of identity, subjectivity, agency, and individuality is enforced by the Pavlovian economics of social media, where every whim and superficial desire helps build an ever-shrinking personal universe, distorting all perspective of what and who is on the other side of the bubble. This is not just a problem for "those people"; it is, as said, endemic to many mainstream attempts to come to grips with the purposes and functions of technologies of sensing and modeling. I am no apologist for monopolist digital monoculture and have spent the better part of a decade formulating alternative models to it, but one cannot avoid being slightly queasy when the press and the academy, for example, reflexively *demonize* "Bill Gates," "Google," and the more overtly Jewish "Zuckerberg" and "Sergey Brin" as part of a New World Order–type incursion into the physical and mental purity of nations and peoples. I recoil at what Facebook is as much as anyone, but at a point, critical theory tips into paranoia.

Conspiracy theory is *apophenia as political science*; it perceives causes and deliberate agents where only truly frightening systemic failures exist. The demolition of societal self-governance through populism in the neoliberal era has left societies both more complex and less willing and able to deliberately comprehend themselves. For many, and not surprisingly, the notion that an absence of viable systemic control has caused this chaos is just too intolerable, and so there is comfort to be found in quixotic mobilizations against alien elites. So, yes, conspiracy theory and pandemic populism are a kind of alternative *model simulation* of the whole, and are attempts to grasp globality and planetarity at once, but only on terms that align with one's own sense of personal prestige and autonomy.

One of the things the pandemic has revealed is that the absence of control, authority, and competency in the West is very real and dangerous. Post-pandemic politics must revive its legitimacy, capacity, and effectiveness. This will be possible only to the extent that the paths toward an inclusive, equitable positive biopolitics are open and active. Those politics will need to remap and deconflate identity, subjectivity, status, and agency from one another in order to build the co-immunological commons. Perhaps nothing is more essential than this.

9
THE PROBLEM IS
INDIVIDUATION ITSELF

Given that post-pandemic positive biopolitics demands greater use of sensing, modeling, and simulation infrastructures, both high-tech and high-touch, clarifying the contrast with existing modes of surveillance is crucial. It would seem that at just the moment when a deeper secularization of societal self-knowledge is called for, the water has been poisoned by years of misapplication focused on tactical manipulation, not strategic foresight. The pathologies of basing planetary-scale computation on economies of advertising and attention-grabbing are clear, but in fact the conventional critiques do not go far enough.

The problem is not that "the system" has captured a naturally free individual, but that our platforms conceive of and thus reinforce a model of society as essentially an accumulation of individuals, to be understood through individual profiles. The deeper problem with the current system is less sensing than *over-individuation* itself. Any viable post-pandemic politics must be based on more pluralized and entangled frames of reference, and the current mainstream anti-surveillance narrative is insufficient to get us there.

Western discourses of anti-surveillance are, well, very *Western* discourses. Foucault's account of the history of subjectivity, identity, and individuation is also a history of liberal individualism, a set of presumptions deep within diverse philosophical and popular political commitments. In terms of sensing, modeling, and simulation, this underwrites the belief that we are first and foremost self-sovereign individuals with innate privacy extending to the boundaries of our identities, and only subsequently may enter into contractual relationships with society at large on the basis of mutual and transparent recognition of those boundaries. This is a recipe of neoliberal social psychology but also the way that "surveillance capitalism" is described by critics like Shoshana Zuboff. After peeling away all the appeals to shallow outrage, "surveillance" is presented as an illegitimate relationship between a private individual and a coercive collective corporation. This is also how law schools may see it, as they watch platform technology assume real structuring agency in political life in ways that usurp the supposedly natural authority of laws and lawyers.

What is left uncriticized is the much deeper issue of the organization of planetary-scale computation around predicting and placating *individual human desires* in the first place. It is a logic that is largely reinforced and legitimated by Zuboff and others' defense of the abused autonomy of the self-sovereign individual subject. The remedy of post-pandemic politics is not to "free" individuals so their individual private wants can be better met, faster and more transparently, but to organize society's capacity for self-modeling and self-composition around a different axis than individuals and their wants. Zuboff's approach actively fortifies this misapprehension: by congratulating individualist myths and fears about sensing and modeling, it may ultimately help *prevent* positive biopolitics rather than bring it about by criticizing the pathologies of the platforms we have.

That said, the pathologies of contemporary platforms are then (at least) threefold. First, their models of people are dangerously manipulative and calibrated for idiotic and dangerous ends. Second, their commandeering of planetary-scale computation for the modeling of instantaneous trivial desires produces negative social effects. Third, the establishment of planetary-scale computation for these purposes *prevents* the emergence of the uses we need from it—which include climate modeling, economic planning, economic liquidity and regulation, and the synthetic intelligences underpinning a positive biopolitics, among so much more.

The specific relevance for post-pandemic politics is that the cramped thinking around the inflated term "surveillance"—an always illegitimate seizure of an otherwise free person who is "psychologically colonized" by their quantitative inclusion in an inclusive model—is fundamentally at odds with the societal self-knowledge, self-composition, and self-care made possible by the epidemiological view of society and the positive biopolitics toward which it should bend.

This is not at all to say that privacy doesn't matter or to forget that real people are always more complex than they appear, but because the terms of debate have been set by the reductive framework of "surveillance vs. anti-surveillance," predicated on an artificial individualism that has otherwise been a subject of due scorn for its analytic and consequential flaws. What the terms "privacy" and "privatization" really mean matters. Not incidentally, this framework has led otherwise valuable scholars into absurd intellectual cul-de-sacs, from the humanities professor offering critique of agricultural policies that require the automated "surveillance" of produce from farm to table as evidence of the degeneracy of the Anthropocene, to the artist–researcher who counsels us that unlocking our iPhones with facial recognition is to be complicit in the torture of ethnic minorities in China. This is not a sign of vigilance, but of language collapsing in on itself.

At worst, it encourages the reactionary instrumentalization of suspicion that finds people not just properly cautious of the built-in pathologies of "the society of control" in a post-Snowden era, but drained and debilitated. They are frozen in place by the impossibly contradictory demands of being *both* embedded inside a planetary society that mediates itself through vast physical connections of information, energy, and matter, *and* simultaneously asked to realize their potential as a self-sovereign autonomous agent with all the associated identities that Western liberalism demands as the precondition of personal actualization. No wonder people think the 5G cell towers are melting the boundaries of their egos.

A politics of coping is synthesized in the convergence of mutually therapeutic chat channels, conference panels, and group art shows that see the need for change but have a hard time imagining the parameters of a truly non-surveillant society—a world utterly self-unaware at larger scales of abstraction—other than as dollhouse set pieces. No one is happy with this outcome, which is because the problem has been so fundamentally misdefined in the first place. It is unsurprising then that the watchword of "privacy" leads straight to the sentimental language of "ethics"—individual morality, choice, recrimination, self-denial—for contesting the social implications of sensing technologies. Technology ethics, as a framework, is thus guaranteed to elevate the most inconsequential voices and divert debates into acrimonious contests between placebo reforms.

Furthermore, it must be pointed out that a positive biopolitics that includes aspirational goals like a Green New Deal at planetary scale would not evade but rather depend upon what James C. Scott derisively calls "seeing like a state," not as an apologetic compromise, but as an emphatic intention. Instead of concluding critiques with dreamy refrains that celebrate the ineffable and the incalculable, political philosophy would be better crafting a new politics of subjectivity and objectivity based on what our collective technical abstractions imply about how our species can relate to itself and the planet directly.

It is here that the intimacies of mediation that hold us together come to be seen not as forms of distance but as forms of closeness.

10

TOUCHLESSNESS

The problem of over-individuation within the systems we use to model ourselves is compounded by the physical isolation each of us experiences in extended rhythms of lockdown. The situation has brought new cultural and interpersonal realities, many of them unfamiliar and uncomfortable, such as the tense choreography of social distancing and vocabularies of *touchlessness*.

How, when each of us is forbidden to touch, can a renewed sense of our biopolitical entanglement emerge? It may come through a recognition that societal care is not only a personal, face-to-face, and skin-to-skin experience, but something that also happens at a distance, through impersonal systems upon which each of us relies. These too are social relations. Technological mediation between us is a principle, not a secondary complication. The solidarities that bind us cannot be reduced to direct experience; they are also found in how we build systems for those we never meet. In these ways as well, sensing and sensibility align.

There is then a link between the over-individuation of societal modeling and the insistence that direct and "unmediated" touch is not only preferable to remote engagement, but that it is authentic in ways that mediated social relations can never be. This is not only a misrecognition of what touch is, it is also a suppression of the sociality of relations we all hold with one another as part of a common biological and technological world. It is a belief that drags attention away from mutual entanglement on behalf of privatized communicative experiences.

The problem then is not exactly the prioritization of intimacy over remoteness, but rather the disqualification of *remote intimacy* that societal-scale health care demands. It leads to the negative suspicion of models themselves, on the grounds that their abstractions cannot represent the only things that supposedly really matter, which are phenomenological, not epidemiological. This is not just anti-intellectualism through the hyperinflation of aesthetics; it is a specific and expensive form of resistance to the implications of a biotechnical reality. Therefore, in relation to the sensing layer more generally, positive biopolitics must collapse the dichotomization of interpersonal and infrastructural modes of sensing. We must see them instead as mutually reinforcing.

Cameroonian philosopher Achille Mbembe and I come to different but not necessarily irresolvable conclusions about how planetary-scale computation supports the project of reason and a viable planetarity. However, on what makes the experiential privatization of subjectivity deeply problematic for that project, we are in clear agreement when he writes:

What's striking . . . is the apparent shift from a politics of reason to a politics of experience . . . In the eyes of many, personal experience has become the new way of being at home in the world. It's like the bubble that holds the foam at a distance. Experience nowadays trumps reason . . . We're led to believe that sensibility, emotions, affect, sentiments and feelings are all the real stuff of subjecthood, and therefore, of radical agency. Paradoxically, in the paranoid tenor of our epoch, this is very much in tune with the dominant strictures of neoliberal individualism.

I would extend this by saying that a privatized subjectivity and the attendant hyper-interiorized individuation hinge on a commitment to the authenticity and efficacy of affect. This embraces the notion that a preferred personal narrativization of the world can, and in fact should, take priority over the cold reality of the planet and its indifferent biochemistries. It is the "culture" in "culture war." It is not only part of the psychology of the pandemic, it characterizes the rise of populism that, now holding on to power, has mismanaged responses to the pandemic so fatally.

Jean-Luc Nancy, commenting on "touch and touchlessness," describes how all touch is ultimately and finally touchless, that touchlessness is the basis of our intimacies. As we view a grid of hundreds of viewers in a videoconference, where voices and images of faces surely *touch* all of our ears and eyes, he reminds us how even the most intimate encounters are mediated by sights and sounds, machines, bodily fluids, membranes, and prescribed behaviors. Knowing what can and cannot be touched is a form of embodied social intelligence. Prohibitions against certain kinds of touching, such as the "touching death" taboo against laying a hand on the corpse of a deceased loved one, for example, have their own obvious "biopolitical" logic in that they prioritize the prevention of disease transmission over the personal expression of grief. His most emphatic point is that we are touching and being touched constantly, and thus mediation is not a secondary condition of our embodiment, it *is* the condition of our embodiment.

Instead of thinking of touch as that which is *im*mediate—without mediation—we understand instead that even as one experience may have more visceral tactility than another, that touching is always to some degree *touching at a distance*, and across a distance that is not empty but full of mediation. The significance of this for the context of the pandemic is in locating the provision of medical care within the larger, discontiguous social apparatus of sensing. That is, the sensing layer is how the larger social body, in essence, touches itself and senses itself so that another exacting kind of touch, which is this provision of medical care, can be provided.

The models that social sensing produces allow for a general calibration of touch and touchlessness as a matter of intimacy, but intimacy in the form of biopolitical self-composition. For example, among the most intimate technologies of touchlessness is the mask. It is not just an intervention onto the individual body but a collaborative technology that through filtration mediates the proxemic relationship between two or more of us. Because we are always touched by one another's exhalations, the mask makes the interrelation a matter of shared concern. It prevents contact by the deliberate withdrawal of the space between us, and it is precisely for that reason a way that we care for one another. Put directly, the mask works not because we care—as filtration is indifferent to affective ethics—but rather we care because it works.

A larger transformation of our cities—another collective technology—is also unfolding according to the demands of "touchlessness" Architects, urbanists, and interaction designers are scrambling to reimagine the post-pandemic city. While they do so, we are amazed at the bottom-up interface design that has transformed restaurants, markets, and other public places. In order for them to remain open, they have reduced their programmatic operations into immunological interfacial regimes of clean and unclean components, plexiglass perforations, and furniture *détourned* into micro-barricades.

The remaking of these sites in the image of the newly present contagion may be less about removing the question of touch from the equation than about actually *reaffirming* it. It reintroduces touch directly and viscerally as a variable that had been there all along, but had been forgotten. This context of touch and mediation between bodies and persons in the fulfillment of social encounters had become invisible in conventions like handshakes, which today seem inappropriate. If before touch was not seen as something that needed to be so deliberately calibrated, that is no longer the case. The *touch-fulness* of these touchless encounters is now something of which we are excruciatingly aware, so we compose the skins and boundaries of the world with understandings we had thought lost.

11

QUARANTINE URBANISM

The filtering and sorting of society has also occurred at the level of the city. Certain features of many cities are already the historical result of how they have dealt with past pandemics, and it is likely cities will be further altered by the COVID-19 pandemic. How so?

Lockdown, quarantine, and isolation are all spatial technologies that filter us from one another because the actual risk any one person poses to another, and vice versa, is unknown. Quarantine is a state of limbo. You are neither sick nor healthy; rather, it is officially undecidable. Unlike many past quarantines, in this case the whole population is quarantined from itself, with no clear inside or outside. In inaugurating the "state of exception," the standard biopolitical critique sees "camps" everywhere and in everything. For this pandemic, however, camps are more like bunkers, each with opposite assignments of keeping the world "in" and keeping it "out," the two oscillating constantly. Are you locked in or locked out, locked up or locked down?

"Quarantine" means a kind of suspended indeterminacy: days slip into weeks. The official suspicion that any one person may be a risk to the rest will continue even after the lockdown rules are relaxed. Meanwhile, our immediate habitats are defined by suspicious new relations between inside and outside. If the general quarantine lasts a very long time, some of these relations will become permanent. As amenities that were once known as "places" in the city are now transformed into apps and appliances inside the home, public space is evacuated and the domestic sphere becomes its own horizon. Where is an office? What is a school?

How we relate to each other is part of how we relate to the city, and we have long done so through layers of artificial skins and prostheses (aka clothes and phones). Biometric touchpoints such as scanning thermometers and QR passcodes are another way that the city decides who goes where, and today some are expanding while others are shutting down. We are uncomfortably adapting to psychogeographies of isolation. In due course we learn to explain "social distancing–compliant building designs." Of biometric technologies, those thermometers are in ascendance, but fingerprint scanners have been turned off. Phones are a lifeline, but facial recognition is on temporary hiatus, as wearing masks in public has flipped overnight from an act of defiance to a mandatory precaution.

For the more privileged classes, this situation might feel a bit less like house arrest and more like a trial run of fully automated luxury capitalism, albeit one that is extraordinarily immobile. One spends life in a kind of domestic cocoon to which necessary aspects of the outside world are brought through networks and pipes, from plumbing systems to delivery supply chains, and precarious laborers. At the push of a button, the world has folded into whims that appear on the doorstep. For other people, the circumstances are much more carceral and the experience closer to something like solitary confinement or, even worse, the sharing of a cell with someone you may fear.

In another way, that dynamic may also be seen in what constitutes the "essentialness" of essential workers. Those whose livelihood continues under this circumstance because their work, well adapted to the manipulation of valuable symbols on a screen, such as finance or education, represent one kind of essentialness, whereas for others, warehouse workers or frontline medical staff, their essentialness is far less voluntary. Even though they may spend a fair bit of time outside the spatial enclosure of the house, the social enclosure and the economic closure of their work predicament might be more a form of compulsion than an allowance.

All around us we see "inside" and "outside" switching places. The barrier that keeps the perceived danger contained (what Agamben compulsively identifies as "camps") and the one that keeps it out and the protected bodies within (the "bunker") may look like identical architectural forms. As far as the virus is concerned, they are. As the lockdown was beginning, we saw travelers arriving at O'Hare Airport in Chicago crammed into a hallway waiting to be screened for re-entry into the United States, very likely infecting one another. On that same day we also saw images of London music clubs packed with throngs of revelers, most definitely infecting each other. The queue and the concert both had a body count. The former is an infrastructural bottleneck while the latter is an expensive cultural experience, but the virus doesn't care. It replicates equally well in one as the other.

Once more, the indifference of the virus to our positive or negative "ethical" intentions for it, whether malevolent or communitarian, is nothing if not consistent. Those in the club are not only there on purpose, but have paid a premium entrance fee in order to be crammed into the heaving mass, whereas those waiting in the immigration line would very much rather be anywhere else than standing there with all those strangers, waiting to get through a poorly designed airport architecture. Those in the former group imagine themselves on the inside, enclosed from the outside; those in the latter group imagine themselves on the outside waiting to get in. One space is "culture" and one is "policy." As far as the virus is concerned, it doesn't matter.

What kind of biopolitics is this? Is the quarantine what we mean by a "viable" biopolitics, or exemplary of something different, the opposite actually? The lockdowns, while now necessary, also represent multiple policy failures at once. They are a condition of durable but unnecessary uncertainty. Because of an inadequate sensing layer, the pinpoint isolation of those who are most very likely contagious or at risk is impossible.

Thus blanket lockdown is invoked, in this case not to protect one population from another, but to protect an entire population from itself, since it cannot sense, model, and know itself well enough to do anything more precise. We are capable of better; we just won't do it. The lockdown has a short-term goal, co-immunological function as it separates bodies, and a longer-term one, to buy time for governance to catch up with reality so that it can develop higher-resolution responses. Even for that, we endure very uneven results. It is clear that some places are not even trying and would rather hide, heads in the sand.

12

STRATEGIC ESSENTIALISM

As cities shut down, only the parts deemed essential stay open to enable relays of strategic items, processes, and services. Societies are pared down to the core functions of food, medicine, and communications. It is less extreme than how one might plan moon bases, but not an entirely different logic of utilitarian prioritization. City centers have become human-exclusion zones, given over to serene neglect. Meanwhile, in the online realm, organizations continue as improvised virtual versions of themselves: telemedicine, simulated sports, metaverse intimacies, online education and conferencing, and so on. Long supply chains were once accused of leaving essential needs vulnerable without backups, but for the pandemic, the real revelation is how unrealistic were expectations that localism could suffice. The takeaway is that while planetary urbanism's lockdown mode is an uneven compression of social life, the most essential aspects of its industrial interconnections—signal, transmission, metabolism—can and do hold.

That said, people have experienced the pandemic past, present, and future of self-isolation differently and will experience the future that it portends differently as well. The governing vision of essential workers and essential businesses, or those without which society could apparently not function, represents also a sudden return of state industrial policy by which whole sectors are flipped on and off according to the needs of the grand mobilization, and that vision may persist. That is not bad or good news in itself. But what was most starkly revealed were incredible deficiencies in some areas (medical supplies) and ridiculous surpluses in others (take your pick). For the post-pandemic world, the question of what really is *essential* is an open question worth asking anew.

In itself, an industrial policy of strategic essentialism has resonances with calls to radically restructure modern economies in recognition of the material limits of planetary ecologies. The elimination of socially and ecologically "unnecessary jobs" is part of this line of (not yet mainstream) economic thought. For post-pandemic politics this may depend as much on automation to transform social relations of labor as it does upon a dramatic decarbonization and drawdown of non-renewable extraction. In many cases they are one and the same thing. Perhaps counterintuitively, the distinctions between generalizing "austerity" and generalizing "luxury" may, sometimes, be more semantic than substantive.

In Germany, professions deemed essential are called *Systemrelevant*, which sounds perfect as a cognate with the English. What makes it clearer than the term "essential workers" is that the emergency industrial policy differentiated not particular types of jobs as essential or inessential, but entire sectors. How a society categorizes its own economic sectors depends of course on what kind of economy it conceives itself to have, and so different taxonomies are possible and significant. The model matters, and conventions have a way of persisting and even reinforcing themselves.

Indeed, the anachronistic model that still considers all of "Tech" as a single sector is exemplary. That stability is interrupted when the model must account for what is essential or inessential in relation to an emergency such as a pandemic. In some ways the unique circumstances might demand a unique model of the temporary economy that becomes irrelevant as normality returns, and in other ways they reveal unexpected realities about the permanent economy and how it represents itself that were already true before the emergency and will continue to be true after it. Many of the sectors kept open were ones that did not directly interface with the public but instead were necessary to support and sustain the platforms that did. The open question is how the focus on infrastructures that are increasingly automated and out of sight will reframe the debates on about what economic models themselves should be representing.

Among the things the pandemic has made clear is that the reality of how societies reproduce themselves daily is obscured not only by distance but by how that reality is still conceived as supplemental to previous economic relations. As Mike Davis put it, "Tap the glowing screen and food appears on your doorstep. Nothing highlights class and race divisions quite like the pandemic, apart from when it's totally obscuring them." Part of what has been essentialized by the strategy is the starkly different relations to the means of social reproduction. Exemplary of this are positions within newly regularized social relations defined by the organizational structure of platforms, particularly where people in those positions are put in peril for the benefit of the others in the city. For many, having their work recognized as "essential" meant placing them at sacrificial risk. More accurately, that placement and that risk were made official.

The compound risk is then not only of exposure to the virus but to economic precariousness, and levels of balance or imbalance exist between both of these dangers. This could be mapped by a kind of matrix. One may be at risk of exposure to the virus because a job entails regular contact with the population, or one may be protected from that risk. One may be at risk for financial disaster through loss of work because the work is deemed inessential, or may be protected from disaster because the work is too economically important to pause. You might be exposed both biologically and financially (or in only one way), or you might be protected both biologically and financially (or in only one way).

Some of our researchers at the Strelka Institute compared this to the "death price," whereby insurance companies pay dramatically different amounts for lives lost in disasters depending on approximate future earnings. What is obvious, however, is that the pricing of "risk" and "essentialness" as evidenced in the paycheck of a given worker is dramatically distorted, and the cost of risk and the cost of societal reproduction are being shouldered by those *most at risk*. Nothing so new here, sadly. At the same time, traditionalist protectionism can also backfire. Recall the Italian paint factory, kept open not because so much paint was needed but because to stop the jobs would be economically devastating to the region. The factory kept the paint coming, but also became the local super-spreader hub.

If they can properly account for intensification of automation and virtualization, post-pandemic macroeconomic sector models will look quite different. They may be filled not with discrete types of industries but of with maps of differentiated relays that cut across all "industries." The mandate for "essentialism" means more than a state-driven industrial policy; it is what every organization institutes upon itself as it virtualizes. Whether it is online education, distributed media production, endless meetings, online doctor visits, or romance, what had been seen as the essential paraphernalia and processes of most organizations— from office space to airline flights—has been instantaneously jettisoned on behalf of the essential parameter of information.

That said, the reduction of social economies to an "essentialness"—whether in accordance with pandemic emergencies, or degrowth, or austerity, or highly automated affluent social democracy, or whatever programmatic narrative suits—is never without its contestable presumptions as to what must be accounted for and what must not. The reduction to the essential, and the re-modeling and recalibration of these operations accordingly, will stay with us for some time.

13

RESILIENCE AND AUTOMATION

Another word for the social economy of touchlessness functioning at scale may be "automation." Here the provisions of lifelines and mutual care are disseminations over vast distances. States are quite capable of doing this, as large-scale logistics has an obvious military history, but in our era they have abdicated innovation of automation in the public realm to private platforms.

At the outset of the lockdown, Amazon hired over a quarter of a million people in a matter of weeks, a labor mobilization akin to a military draft. By comparison Google has around one hundred thousand employees *total*. The significance is in both quantity and quality. Work inside the fulfillment center is an intensive miniaturization of the larger and longer relay chains that collapse production into logistics. It is around this particular point of collapse that the post-pandemic recategorization of industrial sectors as differentially "essential" may turn.

Among what proved decisively essential were automated platform delivery services and their workers. They kept cities going when other means could not. The folkish presumption that digital platforms are flimsier than familiar local economies and likely to fail when a crisis hit seemed far from prescient. The app-to-warehouse-to-driver-to-door cybernetic loop became an emergency public service, and proved that platform economics is not a secondary innovation upon the real economy; it *is* the real economy. Indeed, automation made the lockdown economy possible. For that reason, the fate of its workers cannot be construed as a niche "tech industry" problem, but one that is central to how society functions, and to what and who is essential to us all. Their labor may be more hidden, but the pandemic has made their role in the reproduction of society far more explicit. There is no post-pandemic politics that is not also a political economy of automation.

First in China, during its initial lockdown, and now in every city to the degree it can bear, platform delivery systems are keeping the stressed social fabric intact. In response to the virus, stores are closed, streets are empty, and yet life goes on. Hundreds of millions of shut-ins, not just the unusually privileged, persist in private encapsulation, shopping on their phones and eating what the person-plus-food factory at the end of the app brings to the door. With the automated platforms, waves of system administrators and couriers are keeping the world moving when the government alone cannot, and in doing so, those chains of automation have become an emergency utility.

Automation isn't the fragile virtual layer on top of the sturdy city; rather, the inverse is true.

"Automation" is defined here less by the replacement of humans with machines than as the general name for the coordinated, Rube Goldberg–like sequences of people, algorithms, and physical and protocological machines. The rubbery resiliency of those arrangements lies in how they fulfill key functions through the programming of hundreds of interim little decisions, with a minimum of direct human contact, for better or worse, at a time when direct contact is impossible. The pandemic made clear that the supply chain *is* the society.

Part of the demonstrated resilience of platform mechanisms as urban organizing structures for the post-pandemic industrial sectors is in the paring down of organizations, lives, economies to essential interfaces, but that is only one aspect. The questions of how each of us fits into those relays, the kind of work that we do, the kind of work from which we benefit, and everything else we are in relation to those dynamics prove that the spatial logics of automation are inseparable from their cultural, economic, and ecological implications. Instead of being a peripheral concern, the questions go to the core of what "labor" is, how it is valued, and what social resilience even means. The work of those who are in automated loops is neither an unusual niche nor a supplement; it is essential because everyone and everything is already in the loop one way or another.

The conception of a different social economy of automation should make two pivotal contributions to post-pandemic politics. The first is to decouple the provision of basic living needs from the distortions of real social value that come from employing humans to do mind-numbing jobs that machines could do instead of letting them create, invent, and take care as they would want. The second is to decouple the fulfillment of those needs from egregious ecological impacts. These two must not only align but converge into a viable vision for *what automation is for*.

This represents a shift in the connotations of the word "automation" such that it implies not "autonomy" but rather all the sequences of *interdependent* programmed relays and entangled connections. This more integrative conception of automation has less to do with the only apparent autonomy of any one actor or component in those chains than with their relationships. It also brings to the surface forms of embedded algorithmic automation that automate not only physical labor but also cognition and decision. That is, at certain points within the larger relay, *decisions* are programmed and instantiated into a particular point in the sequence, such that any decision doesn't need to be remade again and again. The deeper implication is that automation is not only something *about which* politics might make decisions, but something that absorbs political decisions necessarily. Put differently, a post-pandemic definition of the political economy of automation includes a new composition of the complex relays and of how they must sense and comprehend their own processes. That is, retraining the social functions of automation means retraining how automation automates itself.

Those potential future resiliencies—social, technical, ecological—stand in contrast with the primary way efficiencies at scale are now wasted by over-delivering frivolous and demeaning commodities shuttled by vulnerable workers. But they also diverge from the presumption that algorithmically automated platforms are themselves vulnerable, fragile, and prone to collapse when present realities suggest otherwise. It is a token of faith for some that a principled opposition to long supply chains dependent on computational abstractions should be maintained on behalf of radically local, face-to-face, "spatio-temporally embedded" economies because the latter would be more resilient come crunch time. Before the pandemic, this wasn't true, and the pandemic has made it less so.

There are certainly aesthetic and stylistic reasons to prefer homogenous village-scale communities to the "alienating" anonymity of the big city. Indeed, there is a direct if implicit anti-urbanism in anti-automation politics and aesthetics. Some may have forgotten that, despite their bucolic pleasures, small towns are also facial recognition-based social control systems from which many people have given their lives to escape.

For example, the petit bourgeois Primitivism of the all-organic neighborhood farmers market stands as a kind of wishful idealization of what infrastructure might be and "where things come from." Although it provides an anodyne experience, its symbolism reeks of a Restorationist cultural politics that symptomatically prioritizes ambiance at hand over equity at scale. It is an aesthetic indulgence claiming to be an ethical politics that is claiming to be a more resilient economics. And yet, the world cannot actually "be like this always"; it is not possible for every piece of fruit to be handed to you in person.

One reason the positive biopolitics for which I advocate does not already exist is because of the persistent illusion that immediate participatory emergence is the righteous means and ends. For some who advise that mutual care efforts are not just tactical responses at the edge of the network but should be the whole of the network, the implied logical preference is for a less-systematic, decentralized, volunteerist rewilding of health care and of biopolitics more generally. To be sure, that would be a recipe for even worse disaster. Just ask Brazil.

14
THE MASK WARS

The biopolitics of touchlessness is felt perhaps most urgently with the appearance, acceptance, or refusal of the mask to frame the terms of social encounter. Masks are among our most ancient expressive art forms, and in times of plague or war they also serve as machines for filtering air and ensuring a personal artificial atmosphere. For the pandemic's mask wars, the mask's function is itself expressive, as is the denial of its function.

The mask keeps you and others safe but also communicates solidarity with the immunological commons, just as its absence signals a refusal of it. Someone's refusal may be many things, but it likely revolves around insistent beliefs in a particular idea of one's own individual body, its relation to others, the traditions that have made it legible, and an equally insistent veto of the news that the reality of the situation is actually quite different than what they want to believe.

It is true that the epidemiological reality of the pandemic scrambles the boundaries of individual and group, inside and outside, and for self-identities dependent upon more stable borders and subjectively determined realities, this is upsetting. For others, the touchlessness of the mask, the withdrawal of the face from face-to-face contact, has made for a different kind of prophylactic ethos for which biology trumps ideology, and touchlessness implies intimacy with strangers, not its absence.

The initial shortage of available masks was concrete evidence of a system caught off guard. In the long term, supply will meet the demand as we venture back into outdoor life. The social purpose of the masks is not only to distance ourselves from ambient viral particulates, but also to communicate to others the terms of interpersonal engagement. That is, masks are and will be both expressive and functional; they not only ensure filtration, but also signal our personalities and communicate trustworthiness. This is not entirely new and in fact the mask's role in the making of social faciality is ancient.

The social technology of "face" is culturally diverse, and notions of saving face, losing face, and disclosing face to the public are not homogeneous. Western traditions of liberal individualism suggest parameters of acceptable identity and recognition that may not translate well globally. Holding the image in mind of Francis Bacon's *Portrait of Michel Leiris*, one contemplates how the face simultaneously attracts and defeats the gaze. The contemporary design of masks as both functional and expressive allows for a calibrated metamorphosis of identity. In this way, one's face may be masked but one's identity is on display, similar to how facial recognition–based face filters allow

social media users to hide behind who they imagine themselves to truly be.

Indeed, the cultural politics of facial recognition parallels many of the dynamics of the mask wars. While facial
recognition (FR) systems can be and are used for harm, as
with tracing apps, the social psychology of the technology
can be based not on how the technology actually works but
on how it is imagined to work. Some facial recognition
systems, such as social media filters, allow someone to not
only control how they look but also to *see* how they look,
and are therefore likely more psychologically acceptable
than those, such as security cameras, that observe faces
and interpret them invisibly without allowing people to see
themselves in the FR mirror. Irrespective of other factors,
it may be that the *feeling* of being in control of the sociality
of one's face, and the composition of identity, takes precedence in deciding consent and the "ethical" sense of one's
participation.

For the pandemic mask wars, the heart of the conflict
is over the proper relationship between individuals and
society, what it means for the latter to make demands on
the former, and whether the responsibilities entailed are
violations of sovereignty or the enactment of a viable
epidemiological view of society. In the mask wars, the
location of risk is contested. Many who refuse to wear a
mask will offer some variation of the claim that the risks
incurred are to themselves and therefore an individual
choice, and that the social norm or mandate to wear the
mask should instead be, once more, a private decision.
That the relevant risk is obviously not private seems to

genuinely escape their thinking, and that fact suggests that the epidemiological model itself is for them perhaps unthinkable, literally or morally. A whole political philosophy is at work here that sees society not as an interdependent biological community but as a collection of atomized agents who may or may not choose to enter into social relations. At stake is the way in which society is defined, with the conceptual primacy of individuation contested by the reality of population entanglement. No wonder the pushback is so strong.

The interdependent dynamic between functional and expressive masks (functional expression, expressive functionality) is itself slippery. "Masks save lives," says a main character in the HBO TV series *Watchmen*, in which the police wear masks to protect their identities from white supremacist vigilantes. Before plague masks became the "atmotechnics" of the gas mask during World War I, the artificial filtration over the nose and mouth, in some cases filled with floral scents that would overwhelm the stench of death, was understood to benefit the wearer who inhales the world around them long before the medical proof of microbes was established. Suffice to say we were using masks as functional filters before we knew exactly why, and the same is probably true of expressive masks, even today.

And yet, to really internalize the function of the mask as a technique of immunological and epidemiological control is to comprehend oneself as an organism in ways that likely do not correspond with older, symbolic cultural traditions of self-identity. Even so, that too becomes part of the meaning-making by which a living society decides to act upon itself through measured reason, and on which the legitimacy of its biopolitics depends.

This clarifies then the arguments by which that biopolitics is refused as illegitimate by those whose "anti-mask" stance is not only a private decision but the basis of a very public performance of a specific sense of privatized subjectivity. Given its alignment and allegiance to the populist politics of sovereign power, at fatal odds with biopower, it is difficult to not correlate anti-biopolitical macropolitics and micropolitics. If populist leaders depend on the grandeur of arbitrary symbols, rituals of authority, claims of transcendental organic community, and unwise feats of strength in attempt to demonstrate the superiority of sovereign power over biopower, aren't the everyday militants of this folk philosophy doing the same?

If so, this raises the question as to how arbitrary the mask is or is not. One the one hand, we see many cases in which the politics of the mask can switch very quickly. In Hong Kong, just last year wearing a mask in public was considered borderline seditious, and then in a matter of weeks, masks became mandatory. The Guy Fawkes mask phenomenon suggests another kind of arbitrariness of the mask, as it was overfilled with and then evacuated of meaning almost overnight. From the 2005 film *V for Vendetta* and the Occupy and Arab Spring movements, to the "reopen the economy" rallies in rural Ohio that resemble a scene from *Dawn of the Dead*, the meaninglessness of that particular mask changed from an already vague message—"we are the anonymous multitude, and you cannot defeat us, we are everywhere, blah blah blah"—to a virtually nonexistent one: "I don't really know specifically what to say, but I am angry and so will make a generic vocalization of discontent." The symbolism of the Guy Fawkes mask is now a symbol of meaninglessness itself.

In this way, the "technology refusal" culture of anti-mask politics is not arbitrary, but a positive affirmation of a worldview that predicates both sovereign individuality and cultural mythologies as truly more powerful and relevant than the biological reality bursting through the surface of those fictions. To negate the mask is to negate secular biopolitics by affirming a traditional alternative for which, in essence, social constructivism is radically determinant. For this, a certain slander must be denied, which is that reality consists of a biochemical tumult that precedes and is indifferent to the symbolic prestige that might be built upon it.

The social norms inherent in the epidemiological view of society and the backlash to them is reminiscent of attempts to introduce Darwinian evolution into school curriculum, where the world is modeled for young minds. It is an ontological insult, not just a matter of contested terms, in that it makes explicit that subjective intuitions of sovereign power and its non-secular support systems are powerless against underlying impersonal forces that actually give shape to the world. The response is a disavowal of the real.

The uncanniness of that bubbling undercurrent of forces, their invasive portent, their presumption to literally circulate in our blood, also gives rise to the immunological hysteria of the anti-vaccine movement that quickly joined forces with and gave strategic blueprints to the anti-maskers. As they stood together on the steps of capitol buildings denouncing their imagined captors, a movement began to feel its weight. Evidence of the *not-arbitrary* coherence of the anti-mask culture is its global reach and pattern, and its alignment with reactionary ideas and ideologues of all stripes, such that even contradictory conspiracies found common cause to defend the sacred, subjective right to believe in bullshit.

Obviously, the range of personal motivations to actively refuse to wear a mask is both diverse and yet also convergent on a specific set of corresponding worldviews. Some call the wearing of a mask "shameful" and a "sign of weakness" or "subordination." They are informed by an activist narcissistic solipsism for which private affective disposition must never be questioned by the crowd, now elevating an absurd perspectival relativism to a first principle of dignity. Some such people have been nominated to play the villain in the spectacular theater of pandemic politics, thereby assuring the rest of us that we are the good guys.

The colloquial name for the archetypal villain is "Karen." This figure is usually a White woman whose interactions with others are defined by a toxic mix of privileged condescension, self-righteousness, and comical obtuseness. The Karen character is a hysteric, with all the associated misogynist tropes intact, but with a particular twist. If, as Alexander Galloway puts it, "the hysteric is the one who stubbornly contests the unity of the master, by 'irrationally' negating that unity, by overwhelming it with surplus, by enjoying instead of obeying, by *slipping from the symbolic into the real*" (emphasis mine), then the Karen inverts this diagnosis. S/he is a hysteric who is in great pain to *negate the real by slipping into the symbolic*, as the irruption of biological real is magically imagined away with the power of subjective affirmation.

Karen's role in lockdown culture extends as well to her career harassing Black people for using public space in ways that trigger her sense that other people should not step outside their assigned roles in her paranoid narrative view of the world. Online pandemic culture was filled with videos taken by people staring back into Karen's eyes as she scolded them or worse, reframing her and returning the gaze of racial and class privilege that certain people, seen as dangerous in the eyes of Karens, have to accommodate daily. In viral clips of her antics, the phone camera's eye inverts Karen's supervisory role. Now it isn't she who calls the police and claims the central vantage point but rather the millions of viewers observing her framed. It is revelatory that the character of "Karen" would come to be portrayed both by the person who invokes police powers to enforce her delusions of race and class privilege and also by the person who stands her ground against the imaginary police state asking her to not infect her fellow shoppers. They are the same person for a reason.

Given that we will probably be wearing masks for some time, we should assume that as masks change, social identities will change along with them. The functional expressions and expressive functions of the artificial face and their modes of biopolitical social solidarity will co-evolve. Recognizing the mask as a technology of intimacy at a moment when other forms of tactical intimacy are less available is to see it as a negotiation of trust. The handshake was a gesture of trust through direct touch and may be again someday. But in the current moment, strangers who offer their hand are deeply untrustworthy. The mutual trustworthiness of the prophylactic mask works for the same reason. Early in the pandemic I recall more than a few people saying they would not acquiesce to potential restrictions on social intimacy as a way of "refusing xenophobia," implying direct parallels between anti-immigrant and anti-virus sentiment. They got it wrong. The solidarity they imagine comes from protecting one another by the means required, not refusing to let go.

After COVID, politics should look to other pandemics for insights in how intimacy can be guaranteed by biopolitical realism. During the HIV epidemic, condoms became an important part of the response to AIDS and the politics of not only gay sex but gay communities. Beyond offering a way to guarantee the continued possibility of bodily intimacy with one another, they did so in a way that was cognizant of that underlying biological reality of one's own body as a vector of transmission, *irrespective* of the feelings of love and affection that one might have for another's body. Their power came from the mutual recognition that lovers may do harm to one another regardless of what they might *feel*. I don't mean to draw too direct a comparison between both pandemics, but rather to underscore two crucial lessons: touchlessness can instill and realize actual care, and the decoupling of affective intentionality from ethical harm is a prerequisite of a realist biopolitics.

15
THE ETHICS OF BEING AN OBJECT

The rapid but awkward appearance of face masks in the West entails an even more radical confrontation with the limits of the *subjective per se*. It makes clear that regardless of one's subjective ethical intention, good or bad, one remains a contagion vector just the same. As said, it doesn't matter if one wishes to do good or harm, one's biological proximity to others will cause good or harm regardless. Subjective intent is irrelevant.

A source of confusion for many is a shift in ethics from a position that calibrates subjective moral will to one that recognizes one's self and body as an object in a cause-and-effect relationship with the world. It is often presumed that agency and subjectivity (if not also identity) are interchangeable, but the consequentialist ethics of being an object (less a subject) works differently. Outcomes are not a mirror of an internal mental state. They are not directly dependent on public demonstration, performance, and ritual to effect physical change. The implications for other biopolitical and ecopolitical conditions, such as combating climate change, are decisive.

The main misapprehension so common in the mask war—that risk can be privatized—is not unexpected if considered in the context of how social ethics is already predicated on moral subjectivity. As opposed to the epidemiological conception of society, this practice sees ethics as the individual calculus of risk, reward, and consequences. The naked-faced do not mean harm, one assumes, and may even imagine themselves as bearing the burden of risk for everyone. This confusion between subjective and objective ethics cuts both ways, in that someone with a positive moral subjective disposition may imagine that the absence of harm they bring by wearing a mask is somehow due to their personal intention of goodness. It is not. To be contagious is not to be a bad person, but it does mean that, irrespective of one's wishes, one may cause objective harm to others. The harm that one person may bring to another person has nothing to do with the affective bond or antagonism they feel.

The revenge of the real arises in the ethical challenges posed by the realization that the virus is indifferent to the moral projections we might make upon it. A viable post-pandemic politics cannot be predicated solely on the calibration of subjective intention because subjective intention is not the only cause of the effects we wish to realize or prevent. This is a challenge to political philosophy as well, in that it demands the conceptualization of *an ethics of being an object*, not of being a subject, which is, obviously, difficult for everyone and insulting for many. That is in no small part because of how many people have been long subordinated into positions by which their social identity is erased or diluted by being made into a human object.

And yet, the private vocality of subjective determinism cannot hold. The extreme subjectivism that asks you to "be the change you wish to see in the world," as if internal mental states *cause* the external world to come into being, is not the solution to neoliberalism; it is its pinnacle.

This shift to the objective has everything to do with the biopolitics of medical care and the relation between immediacy and abstraction. The body as a medical object is a real thing, flesh and blood and tears. Each of us, at different times, lives in a body *as* a medical object. When needed we assume this objectivity and receive care accordingly. When someone's temperature is taken or they are intubated, or their internal organs are monitored by the puncturing of the skin and the externalization of their blood, which is then analyzed for telltale traces, the care is not based entirely on the testimony of symptoms of this one body, but rather on this particular body as exemplary of a larger abstraction of medical knowledge about all the bodies that exhibit a similar pattern of symptoms, and all the bodies through which the virus has passed. That abstraction, the transference between the particular patient and the generic human, is the stuff of both high-tech and high-touch expertise.

This also underscores the role of modeling abstraction in positive biopolitics more generally. The capacity to provide care to the singular body in front of you requires the moment in which it becomes *any body*, to which a model medical abstraction, based on years of pattern recognition, must be applied as care. This is an epistemological relation, not just an affective one. Through the medical professional, it is a model sensing and acting back upon the world recursively through careful expertise that would be impossible by sheer reckoning. The doctor may care deeply for their patient on an interpersonal level, but more likely they are able to care for them because they are able to see them as an object.

Taken seriously, the implications are profound. One's sense of bioethics would extend then not only to the protection of personal privacy and the prevention of the violence of being treated like a mere object, but also to the deliberate and ethical self-objectification as a responsible participant in the model abstractions through which the care of others is realized. An overemphasis in bioethics on the sanctity of the sovereign individual, and the protection against over-intervention, over-sensing, and over-objectification, may obscure the ethical problems of under-intervention, under-sensing, and lack of access to medical care based on exclusive models of the whole and, consequently, limited access to intervention. Those in socio-economic positions that prevent them from receiving the medical care they need may be less concerned about the psychological insult of being treated like an object by medical abstraction than they are about the real personal danger of not being treated at all. For this reason, among many others, the broken sensor layer and the inability to cohere inclusive and equitable biopolitics is itself a form of collective violence.

When model abstractions built over years of expert care and collaborative honing become a matter of life and death, a more nuanced approach comes into focus, regarding both what is and isn't invasive "surveillance," and how a society should undertake sensing and modeling so that it can compose itself deliberately. The same can be said for climate models, which will demand a similar reckoning with a social "ethics" that is not based on coaxing enough subjective moral gestures to change planetary geochemistry but on more direct interventions in a composite condition.

To be sure, the ways that this post-pandemic politics complicates deep cultures of individualism, subjectivism, and experientialism now at the center of conception of the common good, will invite vociferous reaction and resistance. These habits and impulses reside at the core of Western social thought, so why would they be anything but stubborn? One assumes as well that this resistance will come not only from the obvious political right-wing cultures that have hitched themselves to sovereign power over biopower until the literal end of the world, but also, I am sorry to say, from philosophers to whom people have looked for guidance as to what the interrelations between biology, politics, and the body have been and should be.

Behold the fear in this voice, already introduced above: "At stake here is nothing other than the new and 'normal' biopolitical relation between citizens and the State. This relation no longer has to do with free and active participation in the public sphere, but instead concerns the routine inscription and registration of *the most private and most incommunicable element of subjectivity, the biopolitical life of the body*" (emphasis mine). So wrote Italian philosopher Giorgio Agamben. Once more, the "biopolitical life of the body" is not incommunicable, nor the basis of a private subjectivity, as should be obvious to anyone with a rudimentary interest in modern biological knowledge, let alone epidemiology.

Perhaps we should have seen it coming, but what happened next was one of the most cataclysmic and grotesque self-owns in the history of philosophy.

16

AGAMBEN, HAVING BEEN LOST

It cannot be said that philosophy offered the necessary wisdom in the midst of the pandemic that would orient societal conception of what is at stake and how to address it. In more than a few cases, philosophy's response was even worse than unhelpful. From this I conclude that post-pandemic politics must be animated by a different kind of political philosophy than the type offered by the usual suspects.

It is possible that Giorgio Agamben destroyed whatever was left of his reputation as a public intellectual with his many agitated, delusional, and frankly embarrassing published responses to the COVID-19 pandemic. In a series of increasingly bizarre editorial essays published over several weeks, he tainted a lifetime of work. As of now, it is suggested that no one can again quote him without a disclaimer. This is not to suggest that his body of work is devoid of value, but it is qualified by the fact that when a biopolitical philosophy was needed most, the author went mad.

The significance here for post-pandemic biopolitics is not just that one septuagenarian was not a very helpful reference, but that the episode demonstrates just how much work is in front of us and how broken and frightened the Western theoretical discourse about biology, politics, and design really is. For that reason, it is worth trying to make sense of what happened.

At the beginning of the pandemic, as outbreaks first reached Europe, initial reactions were sometimes extremely confused. Recall the conversation I mentioned with the technology theorist who argued that pervasive testing should be avoided because it encourages the "greater problem" that is "Big Data biopolitics"; and who even told his students to refuse testing on those grounds. He went on to suggest that, in the long run, the "state of exception" would "turn cities into *camps*." From where does this language come and why was it so ready at hand?

For readers unfamiliar with Agamben's work, he is well known for several interlocking concepts and terms, which include "state of exception," *Homo sacer*, *zoe* and *bios*, the "camp," and *nomos*. Agamben expounds his model of political sovereignty in reference to the work of Carl Schmitt by emphasizing that final sovereignty sits not with the formal executive in a legal order but with the capacity to declare a *state of exception* during which laws are suspended and emergency powers enacted. He establishes this framework through a study of the convoluted legal origins of Nazi-era concentration camps, but instead of seeing these as exceptions to the normal course of things, he argues that "the camp" as a spatio-political typology is in fact the general *nomos* of the modern era; that is, its foundational spatial, legal organizing principle. In the wake of 9/11, Agamben's work was widely used to explain institutions like Guantanamo Bay and the Patriot Act.

In other words, for him camps are actually everywhere if you know how to see them. The exception is now the norm. What do camps do to all of us? For Agamben, they animalize us. He presents *Homo sacer*, a degraded figure of the human, stripped of social identity, reduced to disposable flesh and mere biological matter. It is not even worthy of sacrifice in that it carries no value. In greater or lesser degrees, these wretched bodies populate not just the Nazi camps but, in a way, all the camps of the modern world.

The cornerstone distinction that Agamben draws between the living person and the walking dead is founded on the two Aristotelean concepts of life: *bios* and *zoe*. *Bios* is a life "qualified" by political agency and participation, self-composition of the good life, citizenship, and individual articulation, whereas *zoe* is "bare life" defined by the animalian status of an organism without reason, without character, and, ultimately, without divinity.

As we will see, it is the ancient association of human biological animality with *degradation* and symbolic prestige with divinity and *freedom* that led Agamben to his unfortunate conclusions as to what to do about COVID-19.

As for camps—the real ones and the ones that are for him "everywhere" (at hospitals, airports, offices, and especially in front of computers)—they are not only one mode of biopolitics, but incarnate its negativity. In the shift of sovereignty from the figure of the monarch or the Church to the legal supervision of secularized populations, the camp is what biopolitics *actually is* in its truest form. The state that administers this mortification is not just an instrument of profaning cruelty, it is a counterfeit moral authority resulting inexorably from the moment the Church abdicated its role as final arbiter of life and death and became, in Agamben's words, the mere "handmaid of Science." Damn Galileo.

The rupturing forth of the epidemiological reality of the pandemic was met in his homeland of Italy by initially confused denial and willful incomprehension, which eventually led to a comprehensive lockdown, which in turn invited the direct wrath of Agamben's pen. In February, among the earliest of a series of short essays was *L'invenzione di un'epidemia* / "The Invention of an Epidemic," in which Agamben suggests that it is all a big hoax, as his readers are now "faced with the frenetic, irrational and entirely unfounded emergency measures adopted against an alleged epidemic of coronavirus." He offers that the whole thing is concocted by states, which have been priming people for this all along. The implication that he clarifies in latter missives is that the "militarized language" of the pandemic is in a way *generative* of the process of contagion and quarantine, rather than a response to an underlying reality of *Homo sapiens* bodies, infectious viruses, and the epidemiological circumstance. We may take him at his word that what is most frightening to him about the situation is this fundamental "reconception of life."

The piece provoked confusion, embarrassment, and outrage among many of Agamben's colleagues, including

Jean-Luc Nancy, who wrote the very next day a piece called "Viral Exception," distancing himself from "an old friend" by saying that interconnections of many sorts are now inherent in our lives. Nancy also recounted that thirty years ago, Agamben had advised him not to listen to the medical doctors who recommended a heart transplant, and that if he had listened to him, he would be dead. The clear suggestion is that if we now heed Agamben's fear of modern medical conception of the biological body, we too may die needlessly.

As the pandemic and the lockdown wore on, and as bodies began to literally pile up, Agamben doubled and tripled down. There were several subsequent editorials, including *Contagio* / "Contagion" and *Chiarimenti* / "Clarifications," published a few weeks later, and then *Riflessioni sulla peste* / "Reflections on the Plague," *Distanziamento sociale* / "Social Distancing," *Nuove riflessioni* / "New Reflections," *La medicina come religione* / "Medicine as Religion," *Biosicurezza* / "Biosecurity and Politics," *Il volto e la maschera* / "The Face and the Mask," and others, all denouncing with forceful, uninformed prose the "techno-medical despotism of quarantines" and the "fascism" of the medical gaze more generally.

He puts a much more elegant spin on themes also explored in YouTube conspiracy videos, such as *Plandemic*, that this is all a plot by the New World Order to put us on lockdown for the sake of it, that the invasive penetration of the body with needles and vaccines is militarization of the flesh, and that the suppression of the affective sociality of the naked face is literal dehumanization. You see, because the war on terror has been exhausted of effectiveness, the biomedical elites turned instead to a more insidious and personal line of attack. "The state of fear that in recent years has evidently spread . . . translates into an authentic need for situations of collective panic for which the epidemic provides once again the ideal pretext." If you were to imagine Alex Jones not as a Texas good ol' boy, but rather as a Heideggerian seminary student, you would have a sense of how Agamben approached the requests for public comment on the COVID-19 pandemic.

Instead of the lockdowns being the result of an incompetent lack of preparation, and a crisis of the *absence* of viable governance, for Agamben they were intricately calculated and manufactured for the purpose of prohibiting social intimacy and the dangers it poses to consensus reality: "Even sadder than the curtailing of freedom implied by these measures is, in my opinion, the degeneration of the relationships between men engendered by them. The other, whoever he may be, even a loved one must not be approached or touched and indeed a distance must be put between us and him. According to some this should be one meter, but according to the latest suggestions of *the so-called experts*, now instead of 4 meters they say it should be 4.5 meters—those 50 centimeters are interesting" (emphasis mine).

The peculiarity, even perversity, of the lockdown is indeed the unfamiliar delinking of social well-being and direct touch, but Agamben and his school of thought cannot accept why this would be other than as a dictatorial choreography of bodies in a camp. What is the ultimate agenda of the so-called experts with their fancy numbers undermining the intuitive familiarity of ritual touch? It is, not surprisingly, about the machines. "It's difficult not to think that the situation they end up creating is exactly that which our leaders have often tried to achieve . . . to make sure we stop encountering each other and to speak about politics or culture . . . pushing us to the mere exchange of digital messages, so that, wherever possible, machines might replace every contact . . . between human beings."

This line of thinking came to its climax with *Requiem per gli studenti* / "Requiem for the Students," published May 23, 2020, in which Agamben offers some thoughts on the resiliency of society to persevere (however well or haplessly) under pandemic conditions. With bracing clarity of intent, the philosopher known for seeing the architecture of genocide everywhere had this to say about online seminars: "Professors who agree, as they're doing en masse to submit to the new dictatorship of telematics and to hold their courses online are the perfect equivalent of the university teachers who in 1931 swore allegiance to the fascist regime . . . It is likely that only fifteen out of a thousand will refuse, but their names will surely be remembered alongside those of the fifteen who did not take the oath." There you have it.

Despite his hyperbole, these are more than the unfortunate outbursts of an old mind at the end of its tether; Agamben's responses are all based in his longstanding, coherent theory of the relationship between biology and politics. Fundamentally, his is an elaborate attempt to defend and revive a pre-Darwinian concept of the human body. This is the essential basis of his affirmed allyship with other anti-masker reactionaries, but more importantly the basis of his philosophical biopolitical project and the core distinction between his negative biopolitics and the much-needed positive biopolitical project. When he writes that "one of the most inhuman consequences of the panic that they are attempting to spread in Italy on the occasion of *the so-called coronavirus epidemic* is *the idea of contagion itself*" (emphasis mine), it is clear where he sees the real battle lines. That life is interlaced and interdependent on microrganismic scales, that the symbiotic and parasitic are conditions of life itself, and that, most devastatingly, these processes proceed regardless of the power of social rituals to organize them is, for Agamben, a *cosmically intolerable* definition of what it means to live as a human body. For him, contagion is the business of the Church, not of its secular counterfeit, the State.

In "Contagion" and "Reflections on the Plague," Agamben provides some practical advice as to how the pandemic should be addressed by the society that mediates it. The model for today that he points us to is the plague that devastated Milan in 1576, which turns out as well as you might expect. The microbial theory of infection? The function of white blood cells? No thanks. Perhaps nothing scientifically relevant for the mitigation of plagues has come to light since then because, for him, Science itself is the real target. He clarifies as much in *Una domanda* / "A Question," in which he identifies the real source of ethical and political complexity of the COVID pandemic and why "the threshold that separates humanity from barbarism has been crossed." He discerns that this is due to how "the Church above all, which, in *making itself the handmaid of science*, which has now become the true religion of our time, has radically repudiated its most essential principles. The Church, under a pope who calls himself Francis, has forgotten that Francis embraced lepers" (emphasis mine). Once the papacy abdicated final authority over matters of life and death to the counterfeit kingdom of secular science, was the road from heliocentrism to Darwin to Auschwitz to COVID lockdowns in a way guaranteed?

By an expert feat of intellectual projection, Agamben finds the essential effect of this usurpation in the catastrophic conceptual split between "spiritual" life and biological life, which sounds very similar to the *zoe* versus *bios* dichotomy upon which his own political theology rests. The fully realized paranoia that this self-defeating maneuver visits upon him is present in his tendencies to defend a notion beyond the point of no return and to invoke the supernatural without hesitation:

> This was able to happen—and here we hit on the root of the phenomenon—because we have split the unity of our vital experience, which is always inseparably bodily and spiritual, into a purely biological entity on one hand and an affective and cultural life on the other. Ivan Illich demonstrated, and David Cayley has recalled it here recently, the responsibility of modern medicine in this split, which is taken for granted but is actually the greatest of abstractions. I know very well that this

abstraction was actualized in modern science through apparatuses of reanimation, which can maintain a body in a state of pure vegetative life.

Where does the philosophy of biopolitics go from there? The revenge of the real for philosophy (continental philosophy in particular) entails an overdue reconciliation with "Darwinian" understandings of microbiology, ecology, symbiosis, and our own animality, even at the expense of textual primacy and ineffable symbolic traditions—all actualities that Agamben adamantly refuses on behalf of his all-encompassing post-structuralist medievalism. A fundamentally different approach is needed.

His controversial arguments that the pandemic is a hoax-like attempt by the State to implement generalized concentration camp conditions, based on the degradation of the human to a mere biological animal stripped of its divinity, have put his and related political philosophical approaches in doubt. The basis of Agamben's call to "reject modernity, embrace tradition" is a political–theological hostility to the biological reality of the species, which has placed him in proximity and alignment with the global anti-mask, anti-lockdown, anti-science populist movements that have protracted the crisis in many Western countries.

He is not defending life, he is refusing it. The question is how much of the philosophical traditions to which Agamben has been attached over the last decades will also need to be shelved. What then to do with the artifacts of Agamben's life work? It is a traditionalist, culturalist, locally embedded doctrinal edifice, protecting the ritual meaningfulness of things against the explicit nudity of their reality: like the defiant monologues of a Southern preacher, his sad, solemn theory is undeniably beautiful as a gothic political literature, and should probably be read only as such.

17

THE EMPTINESS OF
BIOPOLITICAL CRITIQUE

The positive biogovernmentality for a post-pandemic world must emerge, at least within philosophy, against a pervasively negative connotation of "biopolitics" as a force of suppression, control, manipulation, and exploitation of life as vital force and the ephemeral mysteries of lived embodiment. Agamben's work is central to that attitude, but many others have offered much more durable and helpful contributions. A positive biogovernmentality is concerned not only with how life emerges or is made free, but also with how it can be repaired, reproduced, sustained, and preserved. This suggests a willing disenchantment with our own biological, epidemiological, and ecological condition, one that makes explicit the shared risks, disincentivizes exploitation, and actively enforces the implications of social modeling that the sensing layer provides. Why is this so hard for philosophy? Because, as I will show, it had already pre-disqualified the terms of that biopolitics over a hundred years ago.

The post-pandemic positive biopolitics we need cannot repeat the mistakes of the negative critique that Agamben's work helped to establish as a default philosophical format. This extends beyond the mobilization of a sacred sovereign power over secular biopower, even as his own work returns to that dynamic over and over again. For the established tradition of negative biopolitical critique, drawn through Agamben and also other reductive readings of Foucault, the power of language and discourse is not just foundational but ontological. For some this means not just that disciplinary discursive structures produce subjectivities in their image (they do), but that the referent bodies and biologies are *only* the sum of contested discursive operations performed upon them. Like the narrative ritual through which bread and wine is turned into the Body of Christ, this principle of enunciative and inscriptive production of the world itself links Agamben's post-structuralism with premodern European mystic traditions.

This hardcore discursive determinism leads Agamben to rely on etymology to explain almost any topic, as if the Greek or Latin root of a word describing a thing contains within it the essence of that thing's true significance. It also makes him seemingly incapable or at least unwilling to allow that medicine is more than a "new religion" of fake experts, and societal biopolitics anything but the militarization of life. At the intimate level of the body, it is, once more, the critical violence of conceiving the flesh not as a medium of divine symbolization but as mere biological matter that is at the heart of his pain. For anyone to say that the reality of indifferent biology would precede its ritual signification is, for him, to condemn us to the camp, and this is, I am afraid, a maneuver that is at least implicit in negative biopolitical critique more generally. For it, there is vital life or there is disciplinary capture; there is intensive affective openness or there is regimented abstraction and closure. The scenario by which sapient life would act back upon itself at population scale through deliberate self-conception and self-composition can only mean "barbarism." The meaningful body must never be allowed to turn back into just bread.

The irrelevance of the "Agambenian" biopolitical critique for this moment stems not just from its suspicion of science as secular counter-institution, but from its deeper adherence to an intensely symbolic *way of knowing* the human body. It is one that derives not just from a particular tradition of faith plus a reductive deployment of Foucault's archaeology of governmentality, but an onto-theological tradition that detours around Darwin yet passes straight through Martin Heidegger. That tradition coheres in a philosophical renunciation of "the scientific point of view" such that the Human is understood by "his" ontological relationship with Being, which holds him distinct from animals "poor in world," such that ultimately there is no Human as such, but only *Dasein*. The confluence of influences that came to a boiling point in Agamben's pandemic interventions are not only continuous with premodern epistemologies, but are bound to the core with a mélange of European anti-rationalist inclinations that emerge in the evasion or suppression of the most recent centuries' "Copernican" accomplishments, namely the self-comprehension of human evolution as animalian, contingent, and discontinuous.

The foundational distinction between *ʒoe* and *bios* betrays this willful misapprehension. It is worse than not real. The self-comprehension of one's own person, and human populations more widely, as foremost a "mere" biological form that is yet capable of tremendous feats of symbolic abstraction is not, as Romantics and counter-Enlightenment reactionaries have always held, a spiritual degradation of what it means to be human, but is itself among our most precious intellectual and emotive accomplishments. The ones who insult and injure us are those who demand that a realm of supernatural commitments be protected as the zone where the most noble contemplation of the numinous supposedly resides.

The cultural life of collaborative meaning—of eating and speaking, composing and articulating together, thinking and laughing, writing and singing, caressing and crying, exploring and debating—and the mutual collaboration not just of signification but of *significance* are not only things that humans do; they are also therefore things that biological matter does. The cultural and political accomplishments of what Agamben calls *bios* emerge from the physical dynamics of what he calls *ʒoe*. It is *all* bare life. This very sentence on the page that you are reading and considering and weighing is an expression of *bare life*.

This doesn't make the things that we do less amazing, and it certainly does not lead straight to concentration camps. Genocide is not the result of evolutionary self-awareness but rather a violent *surplus of meaning*. Its motivation is less a conception that the genome may be artificially composed than that the traditional communitarian cultural bonds that Agamben so admires are somehow under a *symbolic* threat that is exaggerated to the point of catastrophe. The camps are what happens not when humans are stripped of their traditional qualities, but when they become *nothing but* their symbolic qualities and thus available to be cast as mere characters in hellish megarituals of ethnonationalist melodrama. As Slajov Žižek once remarked, "It is poetry that causes wars." If in the actual camps dehumanization meant disenfranchisement from symbolic value, this says everything about the politics of European symbolization and nothing about human biological self-understanding.

In the years after Darwin's key books were published, European philosophy was, quite appropriately, thrown into a crisis of purpose that led in multiple directions, from Nietzsche's ecstatic elaborations on what it means to be an animal, to Positivism's premature confidence in the calculability of things, to Herbert Spencer's dangerous conclusion that evolution implies both teleological and tautological definitions of the "fittest." For the Western philosophy of technology, the most influential response to Darwin's challenge is brought by a writer who cannot bring himself to mention Darwin by name: Heidegger. He offers a comprehensive History of Being, in relation to its co-construction and resistance to technology, the eventual appearance of images of the planet, and even considerable advice on animal cognition or lack thereof, without finding the then-recent disclosure that that humanity's genetic place in the chain of being could be mapped, measured, and known as being significant enough to warrant mention in any of the thousands of pages he wrote, other than to dissuade us in general from the superficial illusions of empirical science. Despite even this, Heideggerian approaches have proven scientifically and technologically useful in the philosophy of artificial intelligence and embodied cognition, for example. Still, in the coming decade, as the project of continental philosophy threatens to slide yet further into being nothing but a provincial theological dialect, it will prove increasingly impossible to read Heidegger without hearing the piercingly loud absence of Darwin and to interpreting the words that are there as a convoluted, escapist evasion of the obvious.

Sometimes when I think about what might have been, I can't help but feel that in the years after Darwin but before World War II there is a *missing philosopher* who could have developed a different foundational philosophy of technology than the ones we actually received. What would they have written? What if it was a philosophy that incorporated, rather than refused, the interlocking implications of the then-booming epistemological earthquakes of evolutionary biology, geological time, comparative anthropology, industrial technology, microbiology and organic chemistry, into a systematic language as sonorous as it was materialist? The planetary biopolitics of the twenty-first century would perhaps be based on the work of this missing philosopher, but of course they can't be because she or he unfortunately didn't exist, at least as far as we know. Thus, a very different kind of "social

Darwinism," based on symbiosis as much as competition, and a recognition that rationality *is* animalian, is needed and will need to be invented and put to work.

Until then, we can learn from what has gone so wrong. Unsurprisingly, the negative biopolitical critique, vis-à-vis its lineage with the Italian anarchist traditions, holds a special place of scorn for technologically advanced *medicine* and its prurient obsession with cells, genes, organs, invisible viruses, surgery, and, of late, coercive quarantines. For Silvia Federici, the fulcrum point of resistance to this "totalitarian" demystification of human bodies is the active "reenchantment of the world," including the restoration of witchcraft. With Nancy's anecdote about his heart transplant in mind, recall that Agamben recently wrote a glowingly appreciative introduction to the work of Ivan Illich, an anarchist priest known for his extreme condemnations of "modern medicine," implying that it literally invents diseases so that it can capture people to cure. In a cruel irony, Illich died from a horribly disfiguring facial tumor that he refused to have treated as doctors suggested.

For some, Illich's unnecessary suffering only added to his "saintly" bona fides. The author of his obituary in the *Guardian* could barely prevent their stimulation from spilling onto the page: "His charisma, brilliance and spirituality were clear to anyone who encountered him; these qualities sustained him in a heroic level of activity over the last ten years in the context of terrible suffering caused by a disfiguring cancer. Following the thesis of *Medical Nemesis*, he administered his own medication against the advice of doctors, who proposed a largely sedative treatment which would have rendered his work impossible."

What I have called the *ethics of the object* is inadmissible for this approach of spontaneous intuition, folk stubbornness, and spiritual sense of propriety. The process by which that ethics would come to be, and come to be calibrated, through the technical abstractions of experience into model vectors is itself, always and already, an unacceptable alienation. It is not the actual diagnosis that is so bad, but rather what it means to submit to it, given how it was manufactured.

Other brilliant and wise works in the history of medicine, derived in relation to Foucault and other points of reference, demonstrate the artificiality of the subjectivities that it produces. However, for the traditions that animate Agamben, a naive experiential subjectivity is not only *not artificial* but literally natural and sacred. Put differently, would anyone be surprised to learn that Agamben's hermeneutical interpretation of vaccines, surrogacy, pacemakers, abortion, organ transplantation, gene therapy, stem cell research, and perhaps birth control was "traditionalist"?

Their commitment to this mode of negative biopolitical critique is, like that of the blustering populists, a mobilization of sovereign power versus biopower, which is why those committed to it found themselves at the same rallies during the pandemic. Both seek not just to remove the right of governing decision from secular biopolitics but to re-instantiate and protect a pre-Darwinian sovereign body and the political–theological institutions of the traditional and/or imagined communities that convene around it. In the meantime, people are literally dying for the critique of medicine, the defense of a domain of fantasy, and a dodgy, aestheticized vision of science.

In that his pandemic essays broadcast a foundational suspicion of the secular state as a counterfeit of the Church, a corollary rejection of secular biopolitics, and a conservative refusal to acknowledge that planetary biochemistry is *real*, it is not surprising that Agamben earned the thanks of both Lega Nord and the anti-masker/vaccine movements, variously vindicated and validated by the eminent philosopher's learned words. Nor is it so surprising that Agamben's conclusions are so similar to those of the Brazilian populist president Jair Bolsonaro, namely that the virus is an overblown plot by globalists and the secular, techno-medical establishment to undermine traditional authority and natural bodily and communitarian coherency.

The conclusion to be drawn is not attractive. The traditionalism, the gestures to false "autonomy," the esotericism and social organicism, appeal to Natural Law, a Mediterranean perennialism, a compelling interest in the supposedly irresolvable figure of "the Jews," metaphysics in the form of etymology, hyper-subjective experientialism, oddball references to the New World Order, adamantly anti-scientific views of bodies, gender, biology, and medicine, and a general but inconsistent resistance to "the technocratic modern world" place Agamben and his orbit far closer to the European cultural Right than he and they would likely recognize or desire. Sadly, it must also be admitted that Agamben's convictions are foundational to the default stance of far too much of contemporary philosophical biopolitical critique. We read it in the pages of journals and books and, as already suggested, we hear it echoed in the words of my German colleague who told his students to refuse being tested for the COVID-19 virus lest they acquiesce to "the exception."

The question is, how much of a post-pandemic biopolitics can be uncoupled from the negative tradition Agamben and his legacy represent? How do we engage with the tumultuous and permanent interrelationship between micro- and macro-organisms? What are the parameters of a positive biopolitics? A biopolitics not of vitalism, "Being," ritual, and disciplinary capture, but instead of demystification, animate sensing, reason, and care?

That question is contained by another, namely, "What kind of planetary society do we want?" Both questions, in turn, are inseparable from the present social history of the pandemic and the lockdown. They are the driving force of another emergency: the social explosion of protests against police violence.

18

THE SOCIAL EXPLOSION

It would be comforting to believe that all the qualities of the post-pandemic society we may want are already present in the microcosm of the pandemic, but alas they are not. New things are required, and foremost there is no way to realize a viable planetary post-pandemic biopolitics that does not include a redirection of the purposes of planetary-scale computation and automation. That shift must be not just toward optimizing its mechanisms but toward liberating public reason and collective intelligence. Currently, our condition is one of unnecessary neglect: explosive conditions are left unattended for no good reason other than there is no one and nothing driving the train. The massive explosion that rocked Beirut in August 2020, caused by an absent and neglectful government that left dangerous explosives desiccating in the city's port, is not just a giant metaphor; it is the state of the world. If fear is awareness, then, with the explosive return of the crowd, raising awareness meant raising the level of fear, namely fear of one another.

The lockdown atomized everyone, which led to another politics of the crowd that emerged with the protests against the killing of George Floyd at a moment in the United States when at least some of the lockdown measures were becoming a bit more perforated. The weeks that followed saw an intense return of the crowd as an urban occupying presence, as a political force, and indeed as a genre of visceral, effervescent experience. We must include that eruptive response inside our account of the pandemic itself, as a kind of moment of exception within this larger moment of exception.

"Explosion" is an empirical description of the return of the crowd after weeks of confinement under the pressures of isolation, insecurity, fear. That said, the circumstance in which we find ourselves is a slow crisis, extending from the founding hypocrisies of the United States to the built-in self-harm of its civic institutions.

If after a decades-long dismantling of governance there is nothing left but police functions, then that is not only where the structure of society will be contested, but even worse, it is where society will attempt to construct itself. But the question of the kind of society we want cannot be reduced to the question of the kind of policing we want—and yet here we are.

It is possible to respect the call for massive defunding and replacement of police with effective social programs, and also realize that people like Erik Prince are salivating at #abolishthepolice and how such moves to delegitimize the state could pave the way for the privatization of security and violence. What is required is not the devolution of cities into delinked communities but the active restoration and revitalization of the legitimacy and effectiveness of (non-policing) social governance at the scales of the conditions that need governance: bodily scale, population scale, and planetary scale, all at once.

During the pandemic, a reckoning with police violence and systemic racial injustice became part of "the real" that demanded its own revenge. The scope of the year-long wake-up call grew and grew. The mass occupation of cities in the midst of pandemic was not an anti-epidemiological response but rather one learned from the epidemiological conception of the social that the pandemic demanded, as the swarming cells of protesters sought to create a co-immunity against the systemic disorder. Police, accustomed to impunity as they attacked the social body even if, in theory, their function is to protect it, came to be seen as the parasitic contagion demanding a coordinated response.

Any school of anthropological theory may tell you that if you put hundreds of millions of mature hominins under lock and key for an extended period, the pressure will build to a point where some social explosion is inevitable. After a withdrawal of eye-to-eye and posture-to-posture communication, the sudden outpouring of energy for mass embodiment within the city can be seen as thermodynamic release, but that may miss the larger significance. The big filtering at the global level, as fulfilled by the coordinated population quarantine at the urban and regional level, demonstrated a practical capacity for focused mobilization that anyone might have reasonably assumed impossible in our time. Given the inability of many societies to conceive let alone coordinate public policy on so many levels, there is something surprising and impressive about what has occurred. The social explosion of the protests can also be understood as the social body suddenly reminded of the deliberate choreography of which it is capable, and wanting to flex its muscles for additional purposes.

The dreadful homeostasis of the non-future where utopia means good parking and the iPhone 17, in which nothing could really change, suddenly changed. The populist politics that set the table for pandemic non-governance was probably also motivated by a similar dread, but while that turned into a death wish, the mid-pandemic protests instead were affirmative. The unlikely capacity for mobilization was proven. The moribund system could move. Sadly, for many the conclusion to be drawn was not that society-scale coordination was possible, but that it was impossible, and so instead of viable governance, the goal should be *more planless emergence* in the form of anti-strategies like temporary autonomous zones.

It may seem obvious to say that protests directly attacking buildings are "anti-urban," but I actually don't think that is the case. Urbanism is not just buildings but also the conditions whereby collectively beneficial, durable, and occupiable technologies are designed. What is anti-urban, however, is the "insurrectionary anarchist" delusion, articulated by a tiny minority of all those who took part in the global anti-police violence protests, but which, in many ways, is merely the most synthesized version of a more widespread interpretation of the significance of the protests for post-pandemic politics. That is, for them, instead of a crisis of the absence of governance, the protests signal the need for *further dismantling* of governance so as to give way to a direct and unmediated society built on spontaneous and/or traditional mutual gestures. For some, the emphasis is on the imaginary escape from the state, for others it is on the power of the personal act, and for still others it is a convoluted mix.

This vision is anti-urban in that it hates all the things cities are, especially the long-term technical entanglements, the intensification and expansion of supply lines of socio-technical complexity, and the anonymous social abstractions they demand. Its political theorization is retarded and metastasized as the fetishization of immediacy and what Alberto Toscano calls "the spontaneous philosophy of interruption." It is, in fact, a *maximum aestheticization of politics* in that the city is rejected on aesthetic grounds, but also in that this rejection itself is conceived as an aesthetic act. This is one reason why much contemporary art is enamored of anarchism, in name or in attitude, and why in turn anarchist politics eventually devolves into the performative, the precious, and then into misery. The act of "decentralized mimesis" is imagined as the prototype of a new world conjured into being by the act itself: this is not so remote from the hypersubjectivism of Karen, now in a Black Hoodie. That it just doesn't *work* invites not doubt but greater militancy. This fundamentalist faith in the symbolic finds another home in galleries because for some art world norms the curated points of conjunction with anarchist aesthetics allows its own deeply aestheticized ontology to congratulate itself, over and over, for its contrived distance from speculative rationality.

Walter Benjamin famously referred to fascism as the "aestheticization of politics," and as anarchists and fascists co-occupied the streets this summer, both flanking the larger crowds, each found the other like a favorite symptom. What bound them together was their shared commitment to an absolutist aestheticization of the political stakes of the moment and a foundational hatred of rational societal self-composition, all wrapped in the rhetoric of immediate action.

The impulse, in its explicit or implicit forms, to overthrow an established order or to simply insurrect and "become ungovernable" for its own sake (well understood by anti-maskers) is based on the not entirely sound presumption that there is in fact an established order. But in a context where the establishment is absent, the protest should be *against that absence*, its incompetence, and its abandonment of responsibility (and for most protesters this was exactly the focus). "They want to lock us up for not wearing a mask!" says that guy in the back row. But "they" can't even coordinate phone numbers between the agencies that are supposed to oversee the post-delivery vaccine studies. Some panopticon. More relevant for post-pandemic politics, the reactionary populists in charge are *irrational to the core*, and so romantic irrationality cannot be the position of counter-hegemony.

What about the really functional grassroots? The role of local mutual care networks to make up for the inadequacies of official response should not be overlooked. Nor, however, do they negate the need for a viable long-term plan, as some have suggested. Despite the tangible sense of warmth, appreciation, and comradery that these efforts provided, in contrast to the comparatively bloodless boredom of public health expertise, the technical abstraction of the ethics of the object bends toward scale not craft. For post-pandemic positive biopolitics, mutual care networks are adaptations when and where devolution of decision to the edges of the network is more effective and efficient. They are not a substitute for societal-scale public health systems, and should never be a way to shove risk and responsibility onto those least capable of shouldering it. I will refrain from repeating jokes about "non-hierarchical participatory neighborhood vaccine research collectives," but I recognize that for some that would, amazingly, actually be preferable to Moderna having produced its mRNA vaccine candidate in forty-eight hours based on genomic data uploaded from China.

One painfully direct confluence of aestheticized autonomy and political performativity that emerged from the pandemic social explosion is the Capitol Hill Autonomous Zone (CHAZ) in Seattle, where for a brief moment another world was possible, one without cops or a plan. It is, however, a well-established conclusion of historical political science that endless baked goods and lousy music cannot form the basis of a truly durable society. That this risible sideshow devolved on such a precise and predictable schedule does not mean that the modest utopia of a neighborhood for working-class people of all races, with open, livable public amenities and activities, is too much to ask, but neither is it revolutionary. That better world should be presumed, and should not require fantasies of secession to realize it.

Still, CHAZ and the strategy it represents are deeply misguided. In its cutesy handmade-ness, this feral brunch village is finally based in an aesthetic preference for a certain kind of bespoke social experiences, one claiming to be an ethical politics and, in turn, a more resilient economics, yet actually is none of these at all. Its failures are so predictable as to seem automated, and in a way they are. It is based on a formula of non-decisions that are scripted, performed, and, exactly, *automated*, such that the same precise failure is guaranteed over and over. Those non-decisions are in this way the opposite of a public utility, like drinking water, which automates decision in a way that merely seems undecided, and which is a far more reliable heuristic for post-pandemic biopolitics.

The Strugatsky brothers, Soviet sci-fi authors of the novel *Roadside Picnic*, which Andrei Tarkovsky made into the film *Stalker*, wrote in *The Doomed City* that there are two types of riots: "hunger riots and decadence riots." In the latter people have no real needs (other than self-actualization), so they rise up out of the unbearableness of having nothing to do. Now, I am not suggesting that this explains the social explosion of the COVID pandemic, or even the mania for ersatz symbolic representation therein, but rather that it gives some qualification to the eventually overwhelming Whiteness of the insurgency vs. insurrection vs. solidarity dynamic into which things (almost) settled after the Black Lives Matters organizers' initial calls for action.

Consider Carol Collins. Ms. Collins is a smiling, very blonde, pale-skinned woman and a self-described "verbal, conscious channel who has the ability to speak with non-physical vibrational beings." On June 6, 2020, the world was made aware through her Facebook page that she had channeled the deceased George Floyd. Through Collins, Floyd purportedly communicated his feelings about the protests conducted in his name. Part of Floyd's message for us, via Ms. Collins, is "to help stop the suffering, go home—enjoy your family, tell them you love them . . . remove my name from being associated with hate," and strangely, "civil liberties are not what we need to be fighting for, be the one who says I love you to all." Fortunately, the ability of this White woman to speak on behalf of Floyd, to explain the significance of his death and the proper means of protest, did not steer the course of events, though the industry of others who claimed to channel the spirit of Floyd did and will have more lasting effect.

Speaking of White fantasies, if social media–fueled LARPers imagine that their hammy melodramas are actually real, there are also those who embrace the inverse of that idea—that reality itself is actually *rhetorical*. The aforementioned maximum aestheticization of politics is realized with the notion that the explicit purpose of infrastructure is to serve as a flammable prop for journeys of self-discovery and libidinal immediacy. Even more than CHAZ, some books published mid-pandemic pushed the scientific limits of cringe by extolling the self-care pageantry of looting, thus leveraging our inability to differentiate sincerity from parody, and framing leftism as exactly what the right-wing punditry thinks it is.

The lessons of pandemic must be drawn for other planetary-scale crises of biochemistry, such as climate change, and in that regard, some pre-pandemic tactics may appear less attractive in the new light. The antics of Extinction Rebellion (XR), for example, may not age so well. I recognize that I personally may not be the target audience, and that their efforts may do more for people who appreciate their particular style of "resistance," "joyful dissent," and Punch and Judy–meets–*Handmaid's Tale* street theater about oil companies. That's fine. But there is something more disturbing about this format that connects with the excesses of insurrectionary anarchism and represents a negative lesson for post-pandemic politics: the protest style's focus on intense personal experience and the subjective performance of transformation as both the means and register of systemic change.

I worry about the real outcome of a strategy based on the imaginary conflation of participation, subjectivity, and agency. It can amplify neurotic fallacies that are diametrically opposite from an understanding that the virus or climate change is *indifferent* to benevolent or malevolent intentionality. In short, when subjectivity and agency are conflated, then the need for greater agency manifests as the performance of subjectivity. Perhaps XR has done so well as a brand because it works just like so many other brands? It is a politics of mobilization based on an artificial intensification of *identity* that seeks to intensify *subjectivity*, which will, so the conviction goes, intensify *agency*.

The revised project for planetary-scale computation would fundamentally dis-individuate the unit of observation and action. Instead, however, the positive-feedback flywheel effect reinforces individuation and the relentless reinforcement of expressive subjectivity leads to an accelerating decoupling of the narrativization of action from any efficacy of outcomes. The former subordinates the latter. Over time, for those experiencing it, that decoupling and those outcomes matter less and less compared with the narrative. Perhaps this is why the Yellow Vests–to–QAnon pipeline is so smooth.

The problem is not just on the political margins. The pandemic also saw many more episodes of mainstream and centrist imbecilic affirmationism. None was as unanimously denounced on arrival as the video organized by actor Gal Gadot beginning with their preening and looming over the camera like a giant parent, followed by a clown parade of celebrities cooing "Imagine," John Lennon's anthem to unmoored Boomer self-admiration, as a lullaby of encouragement to all the little people scared of what will come next. The emphatic popular rejection of this gift was swift, harsh, and lovely to behold.

The ongoing cultural processing of Black Lives Matter was not immune from this either. It touches too many nerves for it to completely escape the clutch of sublimation. Sadly, it compelled people not just to "say it" as if saying it is what will make it so, but to find ways of saying it without saying anything at all. Consider the Instagram black square, a sign of mass inarticulateness inspired by a general need to say something so as to not be seen saying nothing. Feeds that usually feature vacations and brunch were getting real and declaring solidarity with the movement by posting an all-black image. (Get it? Black?) For some it was a cynical pose, but for others maybe a sincere declaration of a change of heart. Even so, the unasked question "*Why* don't Black Lives Matter?" conveys a more difficult kind of judgment that is not just a change of attitude, and so maybe beyond what can be expected from many.

Put differently, "Black Lives Matter" is a powerful statement because it needs to be said at all. Its truth should be presumed. But articulating it out loud, in the form of a discrete, declarative statement, as if separate from the context in which it is stated, calls attention to the ways that Black lives have been made to not matter, are excluded from what matters, are assumed to be immaterial to the matters at hand, and in the history of colonialism are a site of material extraction. All true. The night will come. It is more the case that the obviousness of the statement is its power than that the power of the statement is its redundant obviousness.

For that very reason, when we hear the phrase declared *so* emphatically by White people, as if the statement is somewhat less than a given, it sounds *odd*. Perhaps the historical implications of the phrase have just now occurred to this person? Perhaps they have the zealotry of a new convert who feels a burning obligation to spread the word and announce before friends and family the truth of their conversion? OK, if so. At worst, the experience is as if someone were to proclaim that "spousal abuse is bad." Yes, it is. "You are right, but why are you yelling? Is it not a bit suspicious that you feel it necessary to let us know that you now know this and are so moved to offer your testimony? Perhaps you should re-post that same list of books people should read and another list of next steps they can take, personally, right now. Perhaps they are as lost as you once were and could use the guidance?"

In this milieu, the Instagram black square may be seen by future AI archeologists as the pinnacle of impotent Western politics in the age of Experientialist Populism, had it not been for the work of thought leader Kendall Jenner. You may recall the TV commercial in which the billionaire celebrity attends a super-important demonstration with all the other young people, and decides to courageously cross boundaries with characteristic panache, finding the cool humanity within the cute policeman, forcing him to drop his character armor, by offering The Gift that settles all contested debts: a bottle of Pepsi.

Finally, most of the above will not work as the foundation of a post-pandemic positive biopolitics. What would work? What is the plan, or least the parameters of what is to be done?

19

FOR PLANETARY COMPETENCY

The revenge of the real is the realization that governance of planetary realities should not be left to a patchwork of ceremonial parliaments and constrained private interests. Ultimately, it includes not just the post-pandemic near future but an accounting with the past and the long-term future as well. It is not a matter of global omniscience or omnipotence, but of planetary *competence*. It is a call for a biogovernmentality that trains planetary-scale computation and modeling capacities on infrastructures for the remediation and rectification of a wounded species and its wounded habitat.

At the end of the day, there is no really good technical reason why every man, woman, and child was not given a test, care, and comfort as soon as the virus was known. With basic foresight, it was possible and it is still possible. Planetary competency is not, as some "down to Earthers" would warn you, a "Promethean techno-optimist dream"; it is simply applying speculative reason and understood techniques to known problems in careful ways by reorganizing social and economic infrastructures to meet their real purposes. By contrast, "just putting it out there into the universe" that the accumulation of apps, horizontal care networks, trickster hacks, and workarounds, or the emergent intelligence of ethical tech, local communities, transitional delinking, or very intense acts of subjective expression will add up to a better outcome is not a serious position but rather a sign of beleaguered melancholia.

The relationship between the pandemic and climate change is not only that both represent and reveal an absence of functioning governance capable of acting at the scale of the phenomenon. Both phenomena are also things that are known to us as statistical models that could not possibly have been gleaned without pervasive sensing, calculation indexing and modeling of the real. Both attest to the role of governing simulations as a medium through which the whole makes sense of itself and acts back upon itself. Just as the virus cannot be overcome with the passive human sacrifice of herd immunity, the response to anthropogenic climate change must be equally anthropogenic if it is to be effective. The artificiality of that response—its "anthropogenicity" and sense of being composed deliberately—is something that we should not just accept but embrace.

The great paradox of the pandemic—that it is, on one hand, binding together planetary society through its peculiar contagion vector and, on the other hand, subdividing and re-filtering planetary society by re-sorting everyone back into their country of passport—suggests that the response to the pandemic should have been planetary-scale in the first place. It should have been a coordinated response that could anticipate pathways and provide them when needed. The division of populations into smaller, manageable groups (like countries or cities) is not in itself irrational, but doing so without effective cooperation between those blocks most definitely is. When planetary society needed a real world health organization that could actually act as a medium of co-governance, populist primitivism and bureaucratic ass-covering shut the door. Medical observation, tracing, tracking, and modeling of the pandemic should have been taking place at the scale of the pandemic itself. Instead, we have isolated, variously reliable, national- and urban-scale models that represent glimpses of the contagion but also the tragically fragmented condition of planetary society and our capacity for self-governance.

I have said that ultimately geotechnology and geopolitics will be indistinguishable from one another, and with regard to the sensing, modeling, and care capacities of a positive planetary biopolitics (as well as deep climate governance), this would be so. They would, in essence, move to a *biopolitical stack*, if you like, an integrated, available, modular, programmable, flexible, tweakable, customizable, predictable, equitable, responsive, sustainable infrastructure for sensing, modeling, simulation, and recursive action. Climate science has all of these except the all-important recursive enforcement part. As of yet, it cannot act back upon the climate that it represents, but it must. Just as a medical model does, it must not only diagnose but also cure.

For any positive biopolitics to be possible, we must realize that the issues we face are due to an absence of control over what matters, and an excess of investment in things that do not. Some will shout, "But they are necromancers administering death!" No, there is no administration at all. They have gone home. In order to unlearn that "social control" is always unfavorable, we must recognize that control is also another name for a society remaking itself deliberately with empathetic reason: it is how any complex, adaptive system recognizes itself and its own capacity for deliberate self-composition. The very idea of control cannot be reduced to an *a priori* pathology, something that "just needs time for what it kills to grow in." Control does not equal oppression; read your Foucault *better*. Control is also means of protection *from*, composition *of*, form *giving*, structure *making*, enforcement *of*, and the freedom not to die early and pointlessly. Ultimately, it does matter whether the administration of this qualifies as a state or a decentralized autonomous organization or a law or a platform or machine or something yet unnamed. What matters more, however, is that it is actually built.

At stake is not only the ability to act at a planetary scale but also the conceptual register of *planetarity* itself: what it is and might be. What is a planet's capacity for self-formation, which is, finally, all that I mean by its "governance"? What would be necessary to actually approach and realize this capacity? That is, what must "planetarity" mean in its most essential philosophical and astronomic connotations? What is it not? It is not putting people and things back in their "original place." The movements and passages of life over the surface of the Earth, microbes passing through animals along the way, evolving symbiotically and parasitically with hosts, constitute a process that precedes *Homo sapiens* by billions of years. An atavistic homeostasis of divine placefulness is neither a realistic nor a desirable vision.

There never was a time of proper place, when the people were in their true positions, when the animals were just so, when the flora and fauna were all set. Creationism lingers in the notion that only a recent disturbance event brought a subsequent state of exceptional amalgamation, but this is a scientifically and ethically inaccurate understanding of the relationship between the world and what is in it. The heavy notion of an original place for people and things underwrites the weird nativist logic that becomes the commonsense rationale for filtering a contagious population by passport, and putting them back into their national jurisdictions. It was as if amalgamation and counter-contagion were an exceptional *variation* from the natural order, and to rewind the amalgamation somehow, putting things back in their places, must be the first precondition for calculated intervention. It is totally untenable for the long run to rely on this myth.

An ethical (because geohistorically realist) planetarity begins with amalgamation as a premise, so that it can embrace the artificiality of self-composition. Amalgamation comes first. Epidemiology is a *first principle* of the social, not an additional perspective that emerges only when things go wrong. This is not hypothetical and, as said before, climate science offers already another way of thinking about planetary-scale computations' purpose based on the predictive understanding of long-term, beyond-anthropometric-scale processes. Getting there cannot rely on farcical tech ethics and regulatory showboating to "solve" the pathologies of planetary-scale computation if it continues to be trained primarily on reflecting the exotic misapprehensions of over-individuated, over-congratulated human users. This is a fatally distorted model of what a society is, and no amount of *political solutionism* will change that.

For the same reason, the histrionic pearl-clutching and click-baiting about individual personal data privacy as the true essential path for liberation from tyrannical capture, as well as the linchpin cause around which the political critique of computation should revolve, will, if successful, only entrench the primary pathology: grotesquely flattening social atomization. The problem is not that romantic, narcissistic bourgeois liberal individualism has been tainted and distorted by "bad man with a bad machine"; the problem is romantic, narcissistic bourgeois liberal individualism itself. Much of today's techlash criticism is a creepy love letter to it.

What then of the platforms we have? Not only do they abuse that pathology; they helped to *create* that particular and weird subject position of our times: the individual as user whose socially significant agency is the "private data" that they "possess" and which might be later "extracted." This is how positions of subjectivity are mass produced. Surely, the liberated sanctity of this subject-shaped human suit is not the hill to die on.

The consequences for post-pandemic biopolitics are

decisive, both conceptually and technically. As discussed in relation to the ethics of the object/objective, another mode of subjectivity and agency must emerge other than "Pavlov's angry clown," which we have spent the last decade perfecting. Furthermore, we cannot just "take back our data" from the bad actors and presume that it can be used for the necessary purposes, because, put simply, it is the *wrong* data. Data about predicting individual habits of consumption is just not especially useful for the positive biopolitics we need.

Here is a thought experiment: you now magically have all the likes, posts, sad faces, and vacation photos of 7 billion people. Now what? What do you do with *this*? Go solve climate change with all the heated comment threads about whatever? Use Palantir's threat assessment scores from seventeen siloed federal departments to build a new health care system? You will soon realize that, given the scope of the social infrastructural issues in front of us, you will need *different* data than what is being produced. Training our compositional creativity on producing the data we actually need will prove more difficult and worthwhile than the easy reforms on offer, but it will require a different understanding of what data at this scale is and what it is for.

The absurdly overextended metaphor of data "extraction" fails on more levels than are worth counting. Data is not preformed and embedded like a mineral, but is produced in the act of modeling it. It is not scarce or exclusive, but rather deliriously overabundant, and the same phenomenon can inform different kinds of data produced from different perspectives. This is the point. When the Soviet Union produced intricate maps of New York City in the 1970s down to every street and building, they were not *extracting* anything. They were *producing* a specific model of that city (for the curious, it is enormously interesting what the cartographers chose to include and not include). Because our decisions about what we include and exclude are, today, motivated primarily by individual engagement and commerce, we are busying ourselves producing data that is largely irrelevant to the models of our own society that we really need.

An alternative paradigm of data may look something more like an *archive*. Post-pandemic biopolitics would be predicated not just on real-time data sampling but on very long-term, multivariate samples of relevant phenomena over very long periods of time. Of course, to a greater or lesser degree, many countries do some version of this in the areas of census taking, sociology, soil sampling, and much more, including even genomics, but not at a scale that approaches what is really possible and needed.

Absolute granularity and omniscience is not the point, nor is it technically or socially desirable. The much more important connotations and capabilities of the "archive" are for us at least twofold. It is a faithful and inclusive representation of the deeper moment, sampled and prepared for future investigation. Second, the ultimate social function of the data representation is unknown now because it cannot be known what will be asked of it in the future. Similarly, the relevance of a sample over a short time may only exist as part of a longer, deeper pattern yet to be gleaned and yet to be asked. To avoid or disable contribution to either of these is to suppress the best social function of data as a whole. Despite the overwhelming quantities of data now gathered, because it is unavailable or unemployed for these purposes, we are today suppressing that social function through mismodeling, which is misuse.

As an alternative model of planetary-scale computation, climate science is also drawn by the methods and ethics of the archive. It is, as said, able to produce reliable images of the climate through the production of multitemporal models, drawn from sensing layers as big as the planet itself, and pushing the boundaries of supercomputing architectures to produce an accountable portrait of what the future may be. It does so not only by producing enormous archives of data, but also by reading the planet itself *as* an archive. From ice cores to tree rings to water testing, it interprets the planet as it is and as it changes, reconstructing it through sampling and modeling the secondary archive we compute as comparatively tiny Earth simulations of the incredible whole.

Of particular relevance to the epidemiological model of society, we have learned through Earth sciences to see the world through intrinsically non-anthropometric patterns coalescing over millions of years. This too is an accomplishment of technological perception. A person can see the desert advance over the course of their lifetime, but one could never see a century of CO_2 accumulation any more than they could stand there and watch white blood cells attack a virus. No amount of deep squinting and phenomenological dedication will get you there. It is a *true abstraction* that is only possible through the extension of focused, secular, technical reason beyond the horizon of one location, moment, or lifetime; it is essential to the ethics of the post-pandemic biopolitics we require.

Per Derrida, the archive is a promise to the future that the present time will make itself accountable. It can also be a technology to ensure that future is even possible.

Conclusion:

WHAT IS THE POST-PANDEMIC?

The revenge of the real continues on its own schedule. As I finish this manuscript, Europe is going into yet another lockdown and the United States has just voted a new president into office, bursting (perhaps temporarily) at least one reality bubble. Meanwhile, Chinese cities are mostly open and back to normal, even without a Mandarin version of the term "social distancing" ever entering into common usage. It was not needed because the strict early lockdowns and enforcement made such behavioral half-measures unnecessary. Looking forward, it is far from clear how much of a difference any of this—all the deaths and suffering—will make for post-pandemic political culture. A different biopolitics is not only possible but available, but that does not mean it is anywhere close to realization.

The counter-revenge against the revenge of the real proceeds apace, until it doesn't. Peak schadenfreude was registered when Trump himself contracted the virus, perhaps during an unwisely unmasked ceremony celebrating the nomination of a radically conservative Catholic Supreme Court justice. The body of the sovereign had been attacked, not decapitated mind you, but the membrane was broken by the alien virus. In the following days, the full portfolio of presently available biomedical treatments was deployed upon his body, leading eventually to his recovery and a few days of TV stagecraft celebrating this miracle: proof of the sovereign's cosmic power, by his word and by his person, over the contaminant.

The ignominious end of the Trump administration culminated in the grotesque spectacle of hundreds of weaponized loonies storming the US Capitol demanding death to tyrants, the suspension of a formal procedure necessary to affirm electoral votes, as well as more clicks and subscribers. Their rage was matched only by their confusion. Many seemed perplexed as to what to do with themselves once there. To take selfies was the eventual decision of many who were not busy brutally attacking guards.

Despite the horror, perhaps the "Stop the Steal" riot cannot be defined exactly as political violence. To do so would be to presume that the assembly was contesting a political reality that actually exists. Given their steady diet of conspiracy theories and high-resolution alternative worlds, it is clear that their insurrection was taking place in a fantasy epic scenario situated in a United States of their own imaginations. The forms and formats of "the political" are key tropes of this epic, but whether power as it really exists was being directly contested is another matter. Can there be politics, as such, between those who not only disagree as to the proper form of society, but between those who accede to reality and those who do not? One can suppose that "all politics is ontological" if also willing to see that maxim through to the end, and if so, then in the case of the Capitol attack, in the dock was not just the reality of power but also the limited power of reality.

And, yet, if this event is understood as a crescendo of the populist-Right biopolitics that animated the ascendence of Trump and the eventual coalition between anti-maskers, anti-lockdowners, conspiracy schizopolitics, and armed racist militias, then it may be clearer which reality and which "power" they thought they invoked in their insurrection. The "Y'all Qaeda coup" and the populist movements for which it was a twisted spearhead were and still are based in the effervescence of sovereign power: that power is held in the body of the king and his word, in flags and symbolic centers. This is how it is possible for the leader's word to decide the (un)truths of the virus, its cultural significance, the phantoms of voter fraud, and, ultimately, the reality bubble in which they live and fight (at least until it pops). To play "capture the flag" in the Capitol building therefore makes sense until they realize that is not where power actually resides. Oops.

The power of a positive post-pandemic biopolitics exists instead in an incipient biopolitical stack: hardware, software, wetware. It is comprised of technologies, processes, policies, and parameters from different actors in a highly contested multipolar geopolitical condition. It is built of sensors, chips, simulated genomes, needles, and sterile wipes and realized by the labor of millions of people. Its planetarity—its future—is, however, in doubt. There is nothing inevitable about its coalescence or its success. Its foothold is tenuous at best.

Its realization depends on many things. It depends on an economics that enables universal availability and inclusive co-immunity regardless of geographic clustering and arbitrary population subdivisions. It depends on trusted data and models. It would distribute risk such that collective and individual exposure and responsibilities are aligned; it would be granular, cutting across different scales, in many of which the single human is not always central. The images of self-identity reflected in its interfaces would be well calibrated to that alignment, fixed by neither a heroic nor a carceral over-individuation. Perhaps most importantly, its functioning would not be dependent upon the moral performance of its participants nor upon the unpredictable reasonability, superstition, competence, or ignorance of whoever occupies a particular formal government.

This list of parameters seems at once both quite possible and quite impossible. There is no technological miracle necessary to accomplish this; the means are at hand. But the international coordination necessary seems from another planet. The online grumblers asking, "Why can't Amazon handle the vaccine rollout?"—a question posed, I think, without love for that corporation but with grudging respect for its logistical efficacy—suggest to me a general recognition that the tragically clumsy government administration of the pandemic response in the West is unnecessary and unacceptable. The massive state investment in vaccine and biomedical research—over years, not months—that produced several almost instant candidates for testing shows the power of states to mobilize capital and direct it for the general welfare. The contrast with all the subsequent calamities is then only more pronounced. What institutions can work then? A viable planetary positive biopolitics requires a restructuring and redefining of the role of the state as well as the expected responsibilities of private platforms subordinated to the dictates of public reason.

I maintain that history suggests that the geopolitics to come is more likely to be an effect of geotechnologies than their cause. That does not mean that those geotechnologies will just magically happen on their own. At this point, what is needed is not just a push toward "invention" but also a shift in the purpose, function, and rationale of existing geotechnologies toward more rational and equitable ends.

That shift will require not the entrenchment of traditional national and regional coalitions into a recovered sovereignty from global influence but rather the realization of planetary-scale political parties, programs, platforms, and policies (the 6 P's if you like). From Steve Bannon's tendrils to the various Green New Deals we see some initial versions of this, sometimes denounced and sometimes celebrated. Right-wing populists organized a global coalition and funding structure to support multiple nationalist, traditionalist, isolationist programs, whereas left-wing populists organized multiple local coalitions and funding structures to support internationalist, progressive platforms. I ask, sincerely, which strategy is more absurd?

Diverse movements, theories, and plans of recent years, originating from West and East, have imagined not just an expanded role for top-down governance but, more importantly, a vision for a society capable of composing itself through long-term megaprojects. Sometimes that "governance" means states and sometimes not. In the United States, Medicare for All is one such example, and, as suggested, various Green new deals are even more ambitious. Both align with a positive post-pandemic biopolitics, which takes as its subject matter not individuals but entire, integrated and interdependent populations. Whereas these two mega-policies preserve the state's role as a primary actor, others may plan for a rather different dynamic of public and private, centralization and decentralization.

Nevertheless, what relates all these to one another is a view of politics shifting *from law to biology*, from voice to organism. For example, the various national and regional Green New Deals all imply a shift in the role of what governance sees, knows, does, and is for. Instead of just reflecting the general will or popular voice, the function of governance is now also *the direct management of ecosystems*, understood as inclusive of human society.

However, seeing this as just a new mandate for what existing nation-states can do may not go far enough. Coordinated transnational planning encourages investment in infrastructures predicated on long-term recuperative cycles of energy and material flows. Fortunately, much of the most interesting work in the theory of planetarity, ecology, and planetary-sensing has been generating alternative foundations for years. Tweaking the knobs here and there is insufficient. Mobilization of resources toward foundational goals is necessary. For example, a planetary-scale mobilization, state-driven or not, should also include the now yet more painfully obvious link between robust public health systems and economic and ecological viability. It would forego nationalism on behalf of coordination, foreground core research, and delink culture-war romanticism from ecological participation and administration.

These priorities take the intrinsically "artificial" reality of our planetary condition as the starting point. Refusal to engage and embrace that artificiality and accept the accountability of consequences, on behalf of a return to nature or a return on investment, has led to catastrophic denial and neglect. To properly engage doesn't just mean XXL project interventions, but is better defined by planetary-scale *effects*. We know this. We *are* one of the effects. Global programs to deliver free vaccines, for example, are only one way that humans have been artificially directing the course of our own evolution.

At the same time, the philosophy of technology has not always kept up as it should. Conventional distinctions between "society" and "technology" (like "nature" and "culture") may be dismantled over and over again, and yet still proposals that leverage technologies operating at the scale in which society wants to intervene are sometimes dismissed as "technological determinism," as if the technical were not the social, and vice versa. A good reason for this is that at least as often as not many such interventions naively presume a simple correspondence between what we might want a technology to do and what it actually does.

Still, the inverse, an adamant *social determinism* (or worse, an aesthetic determinism) that seeks to "detechnologize" transformation on behalf of a delinked cultural realm makes the same mistakes but in an opposite fashion, unlearning the lessons of social and technological entanglement and presupposing a direct path from wish to outcome. Once more, competency does not demand omniscience, nor does it presume fantastic new technologies to suddenly align just right by deus ex machina. It demands, foremost, the realized potential of what we already know and are now learning.

To emphasize the point further, this commitment to scientific materialism and geotechnological biopolitics is not because they provide mastery but because our uncertain entanglements with one another are *not* separate from our entanglements with technology. We are aligned with Stanisław Lem's admonition that what is most interesting about technology is how unpredictable it is, and how its most interesting effects are never reducible to first intentions. The winding history of architecture, computation, vaccines, masks, anesthesiology, microbiology, antibiotics, and more attests to this.

Post-pandemic positive biopolitics will not be "solved" by technology as such, but neither will it be realized without a robust sensing layer, model simulations of an epidemiological view of society that are able to govern what they represent, the mediated automation of social integration, the technical abstraction of the medical gaze, the ethics of the object, and the resilience of steering planetary-scale computation away from the mirror of individuation.

The path is comprehensible, but it is not linear. As the RNA code of COVID-19 hacks our cells, it starts a domino effect of consequences, not only altering the movement of people, but affecting planetary cycles of energy, materialization, expenditure, and waste. This is the ecological principle of *trophic cascade*, by which the agency of one form of life sets in motion changes with an outsize effect. The reintroduction of wolves into Yellowstone National Park changes, indirectly but decisively, the course of its rivers. To stop the spread of COVID-19, Danish veterinarians find themselves culling minks. The conclusion to be drawn is not that global interconnection is dangerous, but that it is intrinsic and runs deeper than normally realized.

For that reason, as the planetary metabolism has been distorted by the exuberant liberation of carbon and heat, the composition of the needed alternatives can't rely on turning a single master knob in the right direction, "growth" or "degrowth." Our thinking and our interventions must instead be based on an understanding of cyclical interrelations and physical economies, from scales of viral infection to intercontinental circulation and back again.

The composition of post-pandemic biopolitics entails then not just the reorganization of institutions to fill the void left by the current anarchy of international geopolitics but, by definition, that we reconceive and remake *ourselves*. It is to intervene on what should be immune from what, what might evolve in relation to that immunity, and so is ultimately to decide over and over the uneven boundary of the human itself. The co-immunity that any biopolitics produces cleaves not just which of us is in and which of us is out, but also what parts of the biological flux are human and what parts are, artificially, excluded.

What does *governance* then mean for post-pandemic biopolitics? We should not assume that its institutional model is a collage of the past, nor that it will get us so far to restage a surrogate debate framed as centralization vs. decentralization. "Governance" as I have defined it, as the ability of a society to model and act back upon itself, is not limited to the traditional state, nor is it exclusive of the state. It does mean that experiments in the future of governance all across the board should be watched carefully for what works well and can be repurposed for a viable post-pandemic biopolitics, *even if* the purpose to which it is put today is unlikable. It seems certain that whatever those are, the distinctions between technology, politics, and economics will become increasingly less clear and perhaps less relevant. The "calculation problem" isn't made any easier because of this, nor is the more difficult problem of "what is it that should be calculated at all."

Even if the capacity for model-driven recursive composition is pervasive, it is not therefore strictly speaking centralized or decentralized. There is no central "immunological processor" in biology; the function is distributed all throughout the body, and my assumption is that post-pandemic biopolitical co-immunization would be similar. For we humans, in the Global North and Global South, that distribution would include the formal ability to form model abstractions from different points of view and to activate or curtail them accordingly. Whether the intelligence functions of this modeling and simulation must be "centralized," as, roughly speaking, they are in our brains, also remains an open question. What matters is that they must be able to act at the scale of relevant events and phenomena, not that the means to do so must *itself* be a planetary-scale singularity. It may be and it may not.

If governance is finally not just in the law but in the *decision*, then decision also lives in the automation of processes both big and small, machinic, protocological, linguistic, and cognitive. The automation of decision making in response to conditions also sets other things in motion allowing them to resolve, cohere, and provide according to plan. For this, as always the "plan" is less the rigid total master program than a name given to the ability of any complex system in which we are included to comprehend and compose itself deliberately. A positive biopolitics is to be found in the agency of the non-subjective, in abstraction, in externalization, and in different relay points within these, not just at an origin point of anthropomorphic sovereignty. The automation of provision of care at the scale of a human population is a machine with multiple path dependencies; it is a million little things falling together or apart in just the right way. The agency in the system is not just whoever hits that first domino but how the falling cascade is set up to reverberate agency along the whole relay of causes and effects.

As always, the best path is not the most likely one to be taken. Yet, as said, what is most absolutely likely to happen rarely does. The near future that we will inhabit if a positive biopolitics *does not* materialize will seem nothing if not *normal*. In a way, that is what I am actually most worried about. That normality is what will clear the ground for the next planetary catastrophes.

It isn't hard to visualize that new normality. We are soaking in it now. The COVID-19 pandemic made everyone into an epidemiologist by choice or by force. The mainstreaming of the *epidemiological view of society* will induce contradictory responses in how people understand their own personal bodies, the bodies of humans in general, and the hypothetical and real experiences of touch and being touched. Synonyms for "contagious" and more obscure vernaculars of risk will appear and disappear in uneven rhythms.

Our long-term responses to the crises (biological, social, economic) of the pandemic will grow around each other like vines. Some people will cultivate sociopathic technologies of distanciation, while others will manifest equally delusional compulsions toward flamboyant commingling. As a whole, they will retrain our mental faculties to the value of biological self-disenchantment but also mobilize many of its least intelligent implications. In uncertain times, stupidity adapts. Stupidity *evolves*.

What will the middle of the next decade show? The hour-by-hour quantification of the status of bodily fluids—heretofore the purview of diabetics and hypochondriacs—will be standard preoccupations of everyday life. Waves of biomedical startups will offer specialized platform diagnostics for targeted psychodemographics, and private delivery services will have to develop new protocols for physically handling the tons of spit, blood, and piss that they carry from home to lab. Jurisdictional controversies over interstate biocommerce will see the location of many such labs in northern Mexico: maquiladora-scale facilities micro-processing the excretions of the subscriber classes.

Vaccine paranoia will mutate and speciate. Canonical Truther strains will compete with more acceptable centrist Sino-phobia after China succeeds in developing alternative second and third waves of medicines, policies, and platforms. Who does and does not "take" the vaccines will become increasingly contentious, as the annual cycle of flu shots graduates from a procrastinative errand to an overt political act, full of congratulations or carefully nuanced compromise.

Increased reliance on automated delivery services will bring an arms race between struggles for better labor conditions for workers and the rebranding of their work as super-essential or easily replaceable, or both. Long-distance remote robotics will allow for manufacturing and service industries in US cities to employ persons on other continents as easily as call centers do now. In response, robots will be abused for diverse political motivations: nativism, technophobia, or, more likely, both.

Automation will recompose the home's interfaces to the urban exterior. Urban architecture will grow new prostheses dedicated to the principles of touchlessness, and design schools will continue to convene studios of serious aesthetic interest to debate this plan or that. Today's improvisational accommodations will give way, on the one hand, to more precise apertures and, on the other, to the only-seemingly more pluralistic open commons accessible only to *permanent residents*.

Apple Mask (NASDAQ:AAPL) and Nike Filtron (NYSE:NKE) will capture the biggest shares of the *smart masks* market. Apple's platform integration of built-in sensors, tracking user breath and external air quality on their phones, will be later to launch because of an antagonistic FDA approval process. However, its tidy integration of predictive metrics with other personal health–related streams suggests that its position is better for a wider market (including China), whereas Nike's array is superior for serious athletes, owing to its real-time blood oxygenation analysis and other key performance indicators.

Per the usual gravitational slouch of history, most of the changes brought by the COVID-19 pandemic to our homes, houses, and morals will not be named as post-COVID permutations but simply as the normality of the day. Those who are able to will attend to themselves with renewed abilities, and those who can't will provide attention as a service to the former or risk becoming themselves the unattendable. Eventually, the epidemiological dispositions will not be an emergency any more than luggage scanners at airports, counting calories, saying "thank you" to your fellow passenger for using the hand sanitizer, or getting your shots.

Fortunately, however, better plans and paths are also available to us.

Final thought: last month, a reporter asked me with suspicion if I am a "globalist." I said, "Yes, but in a way that is well beyond your worst fears."